Quench
The Conflict Fire Off Your Family And Relationships:

Restore Your Lost Treasure

Njikang Clovis Mebinaji, DRE

ISBN:
ISBN-13: 978-4-9910517-0-8

DEDICATION

With deep affection and heartfelt gratitude,
this book is dedicated to

My beloved wife, Catherine Mebinaji
for always being by my side

And to

My mother, Mrs. Susan Tsafack Njikang.

CONTENTS

ACKNOWLEDGMENTS

I would like to give all the glory to the Almighty God for inspiring and motivating me to write this book, which is my first publication. I hope it will be a blessing to many.

I would also like to thank my beloved wife Catherine Mebinaji. Thank you so much sweetheart for your moral and spiritual support. You made the environment comfortable for me to write this book. Without the environment you provided at home, the writing and publication of this book wouldn't have been possible. God bless you.

Finally, my gratitude to Emen Press for the publication of this book.

CHAPTER 1

INTRODUCTION

Family: The Root of a Nation

The family is the most representative feature of a nation. It is the most representative because it is the very foundation upon which a nation is built. It could be debated whether humans are a product of an ape through the process of Darwin's Evolution or whether they are the works of God's hands through Creation as recorded in the opening pages of Genesis. However, what can't be debated is the notion that every nation is a derivative of its constituent families. To say in other words, a nation is the sum total of a defined group of families. This is a universal fact. No nation on earth came out of space. Practically speaking, a nation does not and cannot exist where families do not exist. A nation is simply a reflection of its constituent families. "Show me your friends and I'll tell you who you're" is a popular adage we all are familiar with. In our present context, we will say, "Let a nation show us its constituent families and we will tell that nation what it is."

All the things we have just said above, what do they really mean? What they mean is that the family unit is, or, I should say, should be, the core to every nation. The survival of a nation – moral, socio-political, economic, philosophical – largely depends on the survival of the sum total of the respective families that make up that nation. The family and the nation are so intertwined that you cannot have a progress in one without a corresponding progress in the other. These two entities both have a relationship of direct proportionality. When a family bleeds, a nation bleeds. When a family rejoices, a nation rejoices.

The family is very fundamental to the growth and survival of every nation. Unfortunately, most nations in the world, especially developing nations, have failed to grasp this fact. Instead of creating an environment and laws that will enable families operate successfully, they create a political environment and laws that only favor a privileged minority. And this privileged minority we are talking about are the selected few who govern the nation. A critical example to consider here is the nation of Cameroon.

Since October 2016, there has been a popular uprising among Anglophones in the two English-speaking regions of Cameroon -

South West and North West. This uprising has lasted for at least up to the time of the publication of this book. Families went to the streets carrying with them peace plants to air their grievances of marginalization by the Francophone-led government of the eighty-five-year-old president, Paul Biya, who has been ruling that country since 1982. Instead of trying to resolve the problem, the government sent military troops to arrest, maim and kill the civilian population thinking that their action would scare the people and restore calm. However, that wasn't the case as the action of Biya's government produced the opposite effect. Instability still looms in the two Anglophone regions as we publish this book. When families bleed, a nation bleeds. Due to the said instability, the Cameroon government as a nation has lost its credibility in the international scene. In addition, it has lost and continues to lose millions in U.S. dollars as economic damages as the protesters have shut down some sectors of the economy in their region. And the nation of Cameroon will not meet its economic and political demands unless it ensures that the demands of the protesters are first met. So, every nation that wants to enjoy true peace and stability must first institute measures that foster peace and stability in its constituent families. Any nation that ignores the plight of its constituent families is doing so at its own risk.

That notwithstanding, this book is not about the political crises that many families do face in their various nations as a result of the carelessness and lack of goodwill in governance exhibited by their respective governments. This book is about an issue that is even deadlier than the political situation we have just presented here above. This issue poses a very big threat to the very survival of families. It tears apart, and continues to tear apart, an uncountable number of families in countries around the world today. What we are referring here is the issue of internal conflicts in families and relationships. This is the interest of this book. The aim of this book is to unmask conflict revealing what conflict actually is and what it does to the family and to relationships. Also, and most importantly, the overall agenda of this book is to empower family members and people in relationships take the necessary steps required to quench the fire of conflict out of their most cherished union so as to restore calm and foster a new and better cooperation between them and the people they relate with. This book you are about to read is a "Do it yourself" manual. I hope it will be a big blessing to you, your family and relationships.

What Motivated Me, When and Why?

First, what motivated me to write this book? Permit me make reference to Horace, the ancient Roman writer, who advocated that a topical writing like this one be kept private for nine years before it could be unveiled to the general public (Sashkin and Sashkin, 2003:1). The reason Horace made the above statement was to alert writers of the necessity of having enough time margin, which gives writers ample time to test the validity and impact of their writing before publication since such writing is primarily intended for the society.

What motivated me to write this book are twofold as listed below:

1. Numerous Experiences of Family Conflicts

To be born and bred in a polygamous family is not something any man can wish for anyone. Mine, perhaps I should say, was destiny. Yes, I came from a polygamous family that lived in Muea, a suburb of Buea, the capital of the South-West region of Cameroon. My late father had three wives (my mom being the second) and seventeen children. Yes, you heard me well. I meant seventeen (17) children. We all lived together in the same house. Conflict was something we did experience on almost a daily basis. Sorry, did I say "we did experience conflict?" No, we did not just experience conflicts; we lived in conflicts. It was horrible. But thank God the experiences have given me a continuous passion to solve social problems of whatever magnitude.

One thing I noticed was that our dad didn't know much how to resolve the issues we did face back then. He handled crises not in an objective way, but in an emotional way. Once there was a tussle, someone who got more emotional than the other, talk less of shedding tears, was likely to be declared the innocent party immediately without any further findings. My late father's wives, including my mom, didn't know any better. This lacking aspect was what I saw as *the missing link* to a genuine conflict resolution. This had motivated me to do a lot of researches on the subject of conflict so as to be able to address conflicts anywhere. I know you will find helpful the material to be presented in this book.

2. Marriage Crisis Statistics

Marriages are under attack today. The vast majority of Americans seem to agree this is the case. People today don't have the same approach toward marriage that people had forty or fifty years ago. A half century ago, divorce wasn't an 'option' in the church. People stayed married no matter how bad things got in the relationship. Today, people seem to have a 'take a number' mind-set: 'next…,' 'next…,' 'next…' Some people go through spouses like they go through old pairs of shoes (Hines, 2002:1).

One of the greatest motivating factors for writing this book is the issue of marital crisis, which is increasing in a geometric fashion irrespective of the family set-up, culture, region and religion. Growing up I had hardly seen a single family without some infighting that lingered on and on. As a young boy, this made me to conclude that it is not possible to have a family without some form of consistent infighting. By this I mean having the conflict fire within the family burning on and on. Therefore, at that time, based on my practical knowledge on the family dynamics, I had concluded that there was no single family unit in the world where some consistent infighting was nonexistent. However, deep inside me I was not totally convinced about this thought. I always felt something inside me saying, "What you think is not quite true." I didn't quite understand that until I got married in October 2014. Now, having my own family and having a tremendous experience of almost no-conflict in my family for the past four years (I say this with all humility of heart), I understand that the key to quenching the fire of conflict from burning in any family is "understanding conflict itself." When you have a thorough understanding of conflict, you will live in your family and relationships as though conflict does not exist. This is simply because having a thorough and grounded understanding of the functional operatives of conflict makes you overpower the schemes of conflict, turning conflict from a strongman into a weakling. Therefore, understanding the nature and operations of conflict is very essential. Only after having understood the nature and operations of the conflict in your family or relationship can you revolutionize the latter. This is the reason why I have written this book.

Quenching the Conflict Fire Not Possible without Knowledge

You cannot bring a revolution to anything if you do not have an in-depth knowledge of what that thing is, how it operates and the damages it causes to humanity and the society. It is a big error to "think revolution" if you do not "fully understand what you want to revolutionize." Doing this is similar to a taxi driver who decides to pilot an air plane due to his experience of car-driving. The result, you know, will be catastrophic. To bring a revolution into your marriage, the conflict fire must be put off. And this can only happen through a proper understanding and analysis of the nature of the conflict itself.

The great Christian Reformer of the sixteenth century, Martin Luther, was able to bring a revolution into Christianity only after having done an extensive study of the Christian Bible to fully understand which doctrines were required of the Church and which were men's fabrication. At the end of his study, Luther was bold enough to confront the Church leaders, rebuking them of their excesses. That revolution had led to the Protestant movement, which is still very alive today.

If you want to bring a revolution into your family, marriage or relationship, there is just no way that that can be possible unless the current conflict fire is entirely extinguished. And it is not possible to extinguish the conflict fire entirely until you sit down to understand the nature and dynamics of conflict in general.

Conflict Requires Diagnosis

Conflict, irrespective of the caliber, is a disease. Until the nature of a disease is properly diagnosed, treatment is not possible. Among the over seven billion people who live in the world today, a huge number, irrespective of the level of education attained so far, is still very ignorant about the true nature and dynamics of conflict. The ever increasing trend of conflict in families and relationships bears testimony to this fact. This book aims at bringing to the limelight some hidden aspects of conflict that are, perhaps, not easily seen or recognized by family members and people in relationships. This piece of work is like a microscope that enables married couples, families and people in any form of relationship actually see for themselves what conflict really is and what it does to the union they had built over the years or they still intend to build.

Conflict in The Family Get Spilled over to The Society

Conflict does not just end within the family. There is a carry-over into the society, which includes places such as business enterprises, schools, hospitals, banks, social welfare, security institutions, Churches, mosques, and you name the rest. This book aims at creating a full awareness of the fact that conflict hampers not just the development of our families and relationships, but it also slows down development in the society at large due to conflict carry-over. Therefore, you can begin to agree with me that quenching the fire of conflict in the family is very essential not just for the growth and stability of the family but for the growth and stability of our society, ceteris paribus.

Conflict is a cost to any family or relationship. As long as conflict persists, that family or relationship will not achieve its optimum.

Once conflict is dealt with, only the sky will be the limit of that family or relationship.

The 7 Assumptions of This Book

This book, like any social science, operates under a number of assumptions laid down here-below:

- The conflict under discussion originates from a people within a defined union or outsiders. The union is principally constituted by the people, otherwise called *union members* or simply *members*.

- The union, mainly created by its *union members* or with assistance from *outsiders*, is not a perfect union. Consequently, it is perforated with loopholes.

- Union members or outsiders take advantage of the loopholes to exploit other members of the union.

- This undue exploitation grieves union members and gives rise to a disagreement of purpose, revolt or injury, which we call *conflict*.

- The conflict in question changes the attitude of the affected union member, which in turn changes the altitude of their commitment and, hence, distorts relationship with other members of the union.

- The relationship will not return to normal unless the conflict is addressed.

- The conflict will not vanish by chance or miracle unless the conflict fire is extinguished.

Disposition

This book is made up of seven chapters distributed as follows: Chapter 1 (current) deals with the Introduction; Chapter 2 – A Review of the Nature & Concept of Conflict; Chapter 3 – The Genesis of Conflict; Chapter 4 – The Conflict Life Cycle; Chapter 5 - Causes and Effects of Conflict; Chapter 6 – Quenching the Conflict Fire & Its Benefits and, lastly, Chapter 7 - Conclusion.

Please note that all scriptural quotations will be taken from the New International Version (NIV) of the Bible.

CHAPTER *2*

A REVIEW OF THE CONCEPT & NATURE OF CONFLICT

Sir Winston Churchill (1874-1965), the great British politician, army officer and writer once said: *The further backward you can look the farther forward you are likely to see.* In order to really understand what conflict is and how the plague has largely affected, and continues to affect, our families and relationships, it is important for us to look back at history and examine some of the scholarly literature that relate to our subject of discussion. A review of the already existing body of knowledge relating to conflict will serve as a catalyst to our current project, which is, among others, aimed at *bringing us into the full awareness of what conflict does to our families and relationships.* Therefore, in this section, we shall be looking at the nature and concept of conflict.

Conflict Is a Reality, Not a Theory

Conflict is a reality that had long existed, and that continues to exist in the human society today – both formal and informal. Conflict is not only born by us, it is as well borne by us when we sacrifice the common goal for our personal ambitions. Philosophy and sociology are two of the major disciplines that have made significant contributions to the theory and practice of social conflict.

Conflict is Natural

Conflict is as natural as the waste liquid that gets stored up in the human bladder. Ignoring conflict is tantamount to ignoring the fact that one needs to ease themselves from this waste liquid. And this unwise action will only lead to the suffocation and destruction of the bladder, and hence, the medical unfitness for the individual concerned, and even death.

When two or more organisms interact, whether they are humans, chimpanzees, baboons, tigers, buffaloes, birds or mice, they display certain characteristics (such as choice of words, bodily odor, facial expression, perception, prejudice, etc), which react to create an energy that defines and shape their interrelation. The energy produced as a result may be socially favorable, socially unfavorable, or a blend of both. Worthy to note is that some of the interaction processes that take place around and within these individuals can be visible by our naked senses while others, just like the reaction of molecules in matter, cannot. This invisible reaction process that takes places within the individuals in conflict is what Anolli et al. (2005:1-4) describe as "the hidden structure of interaction." And this is what this book aims at bringing into the limelight so that the people in a relationship can be aware of and take immediate curative actions that will help prevent their union from sinking deep.

As a spouse or member of a relationship, to not expect conflict of any nature in your marriage, family or union is an act that could be likened to an offense to the very nature we are all part of. Why so? This is because both you and the person you relate with do not have the same values. You both may have different cultures, religions, preferences, etc. Each individual in a relationship has their own lenses through which judgments are made regarding the actions of the other and regarding other aspects of the union like children, schooling, discipline, management of resources, etc. This aspect of plurality of values, by default, makes the non-occurrence of conflict in families and relationships impossible. One member in a relationship holds dearly certain values which they are not ready to let go simply for the sake of seeking the common goal. All these make conflicts in families and relationships imminent. However, as we will discover later, it is possible to take out the conflict in your relationship to live a happier and more fulfilled life. Therefore, the thesis of this book is that *Conflict in any relationship will not die by chance unless the conflict fire is completely extinguished.*

As we have said above, conflict in any relationship is a very natural phenomenon. We must first of all acknowledge this fact before we can engage in any discussion of conflict resolution. So, let us consult other philosophers to hear what they had to say regarding the fact that human conflict is natural.

1. Plato and Aristotle

From philosophy, both Plato and Aristotle saw the backlash of conflict within a society and advocated for societal order (Rahim, 2001:2). For Plato, since it is natural for some tension to exist within a society, conflicts are inevitable. However, Plato felt that "if a proper balance of the parts could be obtained, social conflict could be at a minimum." "Each segment of society," Plato continues, "must know the part it must play and be guided in such a fashion that all segments work together in harmony (Schellenberg, 1996: 89)." What Plato is saying here is that in every relationship, each party has their defined tasks or responsibilities. To keep the union healthy and free from conflicts, both parties must perform their respective tasks. Only by so doing can there be serenity and order in the union.

2. Thomas Hobbes (1588-1679) & John Locke (1632-1704)

The social contract theories of Thomas Hobbes and John Locke suggest that in social relations, strife between humans is not absent, and that the role of the government is therefore to reduce such strife by establishing order without which there would be constant chaos (Rahim, 2001:3). For Lourenco and Glidewell (1975: 489), Hobbes saw humans as "egotistical, the dupes of error, the slaves of sin, of passion, and of fear. Persons are their own enemies, or the enemies of others, or both."

It is important to note that, Sipka writes, both:

> Hobbes and Locke had an extraordinary sensitivity to the dangers of social conflict and sought, through government, to control it as much as possible….not only did these men not see a growth or re-constructive potential in social conflict, but they considered it a flaw in the body politic…. Though neither man insists that all conflict is to be removed, it is clear that this is their intention (Sipka, 1969: 15-16).

3. Elton Mayo (1880-1949)

Moving to the discipline of sociological sciences, we encounter the Australian-born sociologist and organization theorist, Elton Mayo, whose works revolutionized the social conflict theory and brought about the human relations movement. To improve union effectiveness, Mayo stressed, cooperation is necessary. Mayo saw social conflict as an evil that hampers union effectiveness and therefore advocated that conflict be minimized or eliminated altogether, if possible (Rahim, 2001:6).

DEFINING CONFLICT

The number of things couples can argue and fight about is
unlimited. There are the standard issues like money, sex,
love (as in 'Do you love me?'), affairs, children, relatives,
work schedules, roles in and out of the house, reliability
and trustworthiness, vacations, politics, beliefs, and so
forth. Each couple has its own creative way of discovering
twists and turns in these issues (Richardson, 2010:3).

It may not surprise you to know that many authors differ in how they
view and define conflict. Lewis Coser views conflict as "a struggle
over values and claims to scarce status, power, and resources, a
struggle in which the aims of opponents are to neutralize, injure, or
eliminate rivals" (Avruch, 1998:24); De Dreu, Beersma, Wall, Callister
and others view conflict as the perception of differences and
opposition in beliefs and values between an individual or group and
another individual or group (De Dreu & Beersma, 2005:106; Wall &
Callister, 1995).

For Fink (1968), conflict is "any social situation or process in which
two or more social entities are linked by at least one form of
antagonistic psychological relation or at least one form of
antagonistic interaction" (Nicotera, 1995:5). To add to these, we can
define conflict as a situation whereby a member of a union uses a

socio-cultural advantage to suppress or oppress another member who is deemed to be in a position of rivalry in actual or potential form.

However, our working definition for conflict shall be stated as follows: *Any event that takes place within an established union and that subjects a member or group of members of that union either mentally, psychologically or physically to an extreme feeling of rejection, dejection, unjustness, bias, or abuse, and which potentially hinders the relationship and progress of the member or group of members towards achieving the common goal of the union.*

Glancing through the manuscript of "Leading through Conflict" by Mark Gerzon, a senior sales manager of a world-renown computer company said he was not quite interested in Gerzon's book because he thought that conflict was not an issue in their company. When asked how that was possible and how he did define conflict, the executive said, conflict is "people shouting and calling each other names." Then turning towards Gerzon, the executive asks, "How do you define conflict?" "Conflict," Gerzon replies, "is anything that results in chronic inefficiency for the system of which it is a part." Because this definition was functional and task-oriented, it allowed the executive grasp the integral nature of conflict and relate to it vividly like never before. Having been enlightened, the executive then confessed of several off-the-scene conflicts that had been taking place in their company, which they had ignored (Gerzon, 2006:34).

Do Not Ignore Conflict, Tackle It

Many people go into marriage with the hope that they have a fall-back plan – divorce. When people get into marriage with the possibility of divorce at the back of their mind, they have failed even before they started. They will mistakenly see the emergence of every conflict in their home as an invitation of divorce. This is not so.

Most people in a relationship are yet to grasp the integral nature of conflicts, their causes and consequences on the growth of their union. Some have even turned a blind eye to specific conflicts to the detriment of the union's success. When conflicts are ignored, the affected parties, and, hence, the rest of the members of the union together with the union itself, suffer.

Last, in this section we shall look at two of the four types of conflict that exist.

TYPES OF CONFLICT

Generally, there are four types of conflicts. These are: *intrapersonal, interpersonal, intragroup,* and *intergroup conflicts* (Rahim, 2001:23). We shall briefly explain the first two – intrapersonal and interpersonal – since they constitute the conflicts experienced in families and relationships.

1. Intrapersonal Conflict

Also known as *intraindividual* or *intrapsychic conflict,* this category of conflict is used to describe conflict that occurs within an individual. Such a conflict occurs when an individual is torn between incompatible goals (Coombs and Avrunin, 1983: 7). It may occur, for example, when a worker is assigned to a task that does not represent their area of expertise, goals, or values of interests (Rahim, 2001:23). Conflicts that fall within this category are often hard to trace and therefore hard to resolve. However, they provide important guidelines to tackling other forms of conflicts. Understanding the plight of an individual and the conditions that must be in place for the conflict within that individual to be deescalated has valuable applications to conflicts between individuals (Coombs & Avrunin, 1988:11).

2. Interpersonal Conflict

This type of conflict is the one that occurs between two people having a common goal. If you had read a few job advertisements, or attended some interviews, you should have realized by now that among the requirements expected from potential job candidates, good *interpersonal skills* are often stressed the most. The emphasis on interpersonal skills is not just for formality sake. Rather, companies have increasingly become conscious of the impact of these skills in the day-to-day affairs of their businesses.

Also known as *dyadic conflict,* interpersonal conflicts are those conflicts that occur between two or more individuals occupying the same or different levels of organizational hierarchy. Conflicts between a husband and wife, for example, and those involving any two individuals in an organized system, fall under this category.

CHAPTER 3

THE GENESIS OF CONFLICT

THE COMFORT ZONE THEORY

While the primary ingredients in any conflict are the individuals involved, conflicts tend to spring from the same litany of sources for all people, and virtually every conflict begins with someone or something violating an individual's "comfort zone."

Each of us defines our "comfort zone" by erecting limits on what we perceive to be acceptable, allowable, "safe" experiences and behaviors. Any event that intrudes, threatens or assaults our comfort zone, or requires us to move beyond the limits of our comfort zone, produces conflict. Our first awareness of conflict comes from the feelings that are produced when the comfort zone is

22

violated (Cowan, 2003:13).

The concept of "comfort zone" has a very profound significance to the animal class in general, and to us humans, in particular. As we grow from infancy through adolescence to adulthood in our respective communities, and as we study along in various public, private, and religious institutions, and hang around with various people, we embrace certain values we so much cherish while rejecting those we find strange and unfriendly. The set of values we have embraced over the years has come to shape and define our personality today – who we really are - which in other words could be collectively described as our *comfort zone*. "The stronger the belief or the more important the value," Cowan writes, "the greater the discomfort and attendant conflict (Cowan, 2003:15)."

As we communicate and engage with our spouse, fiancé, siblings, children and others within an established relationship, especially those from an entirely different background, we keep a keen watch on our comfort zone. Anyone who makes an attempt to forcefully hijack us away from our comfort zone by either influencing or forcing us act in ways not prescribed by our comfort zone is immediately perceived as an enemy. As such, such a person must be dealt with or avoided altogether.

In my experience and study of organizational behavior, I have discovered that, among others, people have three key values they treasure dearly such that when one of these is violated, the person somehow becomes emotionally displaced, which may lead to depression if appropriate care is not taken. These three constitute the Green Light Zone of the member in relationship. They are, in ascending order:

(1) **D**ialogue   (2) **A**utonomy   (3) **R**ecognition.

For simplicity, these will be collectively referred to as "the DAR Principle."

An Individual's Sensitive Zone

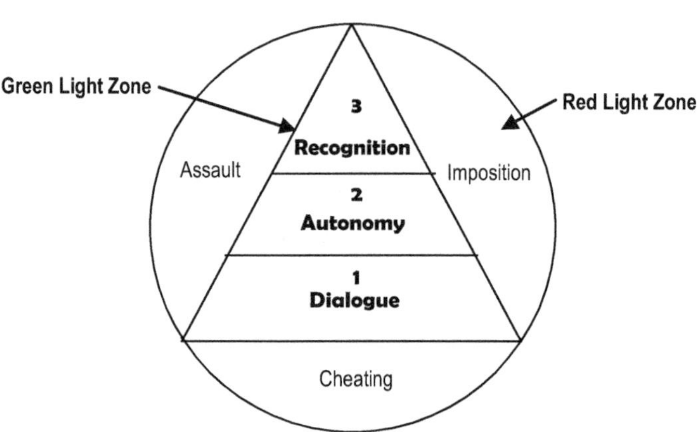

As demonstrated in the chart above, every person in a relationship has a sensitive zone as far as the relationship is concerned. An individual's sensitive zone is made up of two main areas. At the centre you have "the Green Light Zone" and at the periphery you have "the Red Light Zone," the set of three arcs. At the individual's Green Light Zone lies three key values, which, when respected, will

always boost the relationship and catapult it to a new height –
Dialogue, Autonomy and Recognition. Collectively, these three are
the most treasured and sought after by the individuals in relationship.
They give an individual a "sense of belonging" in the union. I refer to
them as the DAR Principle. The DAR Principle states that for every
relationship to last and be free from conflicts either in the present or
future, the needs of dialogue, autonomy and recognition of each
individual must be respected.

Note that the Red Light (or Discomfort) Zone is the exact opposite
of the Green Light (or Comfort) Zone. These two are inversely
proportional to each other. When the comfort in a relationship
decreases, the discomfort increases. And when the discomfort
increases, the relationship itself decreases and is eventually brought to
its terminal through divorce or the willful execution of one or both
parties.

THE GREEN LIGHT ZONE

1. Dialogue

At the base of an individual's Green Light Zone lies the need of
dialogue. Every person in a relationship uses this echelon as a
primary determinant to judge whether they are loved and accepted as
"coequal" by their fellow partner in relationship. By "coequal" we do

not mean that the individuals have the same functions or hold the same office within the established relationship. What we mean here is that though they occupy different offices, one party should not perceive the other's office as being inferior to theirs. Harboring such an attitude will only trigger an individual to place themselves above their counterpart thereby straining any collaboration for an effective dialogue.

By definition, one man can never form a relationship. A relationship can only be formed by two or more people. The word "relationship" comes from the verb "to relate." According to the Merriam Webster's dictionary, "to relate" means "to give an account of" or "to have or establish a relationship the way a child relates to a teacher." Therefore, for any relationship to be formed dialogue is non-negotiable. It takes the dialogue of any two individuals to form a relationship. Still, it takes the same dialogue to maintain (or dissolve) that relationship. Dialogue is the primary raw material needed for the construction of any relationship. The stronger the dialogue, the stronger the relationship, and vice-versa. When dialogue fails, the relationship crashes. Each individual in a relationship must therefore acknowledge this: Dialogue was the reason you sought to come together (to end loneliness), dialogue was the reason you finally came together (to form the present union), and dialogue is the reason for which the union exists.

Therefore, whenever you betray dialogue, you are betraying your very reason for forming the union in the first place. You are betraying your own self. And such an attitude cannot be likened to anything other than hypocrisy. Having seen the importance of dialogue in a relationship, my advice is that if you know you cannot confidently engage in a dialogue with someone, it is advisable not to waste their (and your) precious time in creating something you know won't last. This is very crucial in the area of marriage. The need of dialogue is very fundamental in building not just a marriage or family but it is very fundamental in building relationships in general. Note that the individuals in relationship are very sensitive when it comes to the absence of dialogue. No one will tell you point blank that you avoid talking to them. They will simply react by gradually pulling themselves away from you.

When a spouse, child, sibling or relative, for example, realizes that they are always left alone while other members of the union get along so well, they feel a deep sense of rejection from the union. Sooner or later, the union member concerned gradually develops a negative feeling towards other members for violating their *dialogue* comfort zone. This seems to be a natural process that occurs within every person in a union who experiences dialogue-related isolation irrespective of whether those who perpetrate such a violation are aware or not.

This aspect is true in any form of relationship where there is cooperation of assignment. I came to realize that this theory holds true even in business organizations. One thing I discovered in one of my researches was that even workers who hardly talk to people hold this need in high esteem. One day, I decided to initiate a casual dialogue with a coworker who was an introvert working in another unit of our department. Both of us had met several times without having any amicable discussion. To my greatest astonishment, the person I thought was reserved almost sounded to me like a Sunday school teacher as he began briefing and advising me on how to deal with certain work processes that I had limited knowledge of. The conversation I thought would end in a "Hello-Hello" fashion ended up in a warm and exciting way. That was because someone's comfort zone was respected when he was talked to. So, when we make it a habit to engage in a frank and casual dialogue with those within our circles of relationship, we make them feel at home and wanted in the union. This boosts their morale and prevents potential conflicts.

2. Autonomy

The need to be in control means the need to feel like we are in control of ourselves and our destiny – that we have options, and that we are free and able to make choices. Whenever we sense that we are, or are about to be, out of control, we experience discomfort proportional to the extent of the loss. Severe discomfort and, consequently, intense conflict can result (Cowan, 2003:14).

The need to be in control, otherwise called *autonomy,* is the second in terms of value to the individuals in relationship. However, it seems to be the most sensitive of the three. The person in relationship can move on when their dialogue need is violated, but as soon as their autonomy is tempered with, there is a swift physical reaction that takes place within or on the outside. This reaction can either take the form of verbal agitations or a sudden change of mood.

The Divine Command to Rule

It should be noted that every human being that is born into this world carries within themselves an innate "desire to rule." So, when this desire is tempered with, the person concerned feels less of themselves as a human being, they feel unfulfilled. For them, to be *a human* means "to rule," for this is the very purpose for which the human race was created. Therefore, the more territories we can rule or have control of, the more proud we feel to be *humans*. This fact is very fundamental in human beings. Take a little baby, for instance. As young as that baby is, the baby always wants to have total control over the things he does. They do not want any intruder, they do not want anyone to help them unless in situations where they find themselves helpless.

So, when the very aspect that reminds a person why they were created is under threat, you do not expect them to feel any proud of themselves as a human. These individuals will always feel dehumanized as a result of being marginalized. As a consequence, they shrink into themselves as a snail shrinks into its shell after coming into contact with a predator. And the next course of action to be taken by the snail when it comes out of its shell is to flee from that environment with immediate effect into a safer one. And this is what happens when a husband does not give his wife some opportunities to make certain decisions regarding family matters.

If we turn to the Christian bible, we will see that after God had created the first man and woman, God charged them both to rule over every other thing He (God) had created. So, both the man and the woman were created to rule as shown in Genesis 1:27-28 here-below:

> "So God created mankind in his own image, in the image of God he created them; male and female he created them. God blessed them and said to them, 'Be fruitful and increase in number; fill the earth and subdue it. Rule over the fish in the sea and the birds in the sky and over every living creature that moves on the ground."

Note that the man and the woman were never commanded to subdue each other. What they were commanded to subdue was the earth. That is, to subdue every other thing God had created on the earth. The error most people in relationships, especially married couples, make is trying to subdue each other.

First of all, what does "subdue" mean? Merriam Webster defines "subdue" to mean "to conquer and bring into subjection." To put it in other words, to subdue something means to bring something that was not formerly under one's control to be under their control through the application of force. The husband's goal in a relationship is not to conquer his wife, and vice-versa. So, when a husband tries to "subdue" or "conquer" his wife or the wife tries to do the same to her husband, they are breaking God's law of creation. And what you'll expect is for the consequences to follow.

As a husband, any attempt to shun or shut down your wife from managing resources (whether family-based or beyond) will create a big conflict in your family. As we have just explained here-above, your action of shutting down your wife will make your wife perceive you as a predator. As a natural animal response to predators, she would virtually shrink into herself only to run away from you into a safe environment when she recovers. And even if you go look for her in her new safe environment, perceiving you from afar, she would likely flee into a safer environment where you will hardly find her again. This aspect has led to many broken homes today.

My experience of working with people from different nationalities, race, gender, and age groups in the past fifteen years has revealed one common predominant factor: *the need to be in control of oneself and one's operations*. And this principle seems to hold true even in circumstances when the worker is incompetent in handling basic elements of organizational operations. In order to abide in their autonomy Green

Light Zone, most employees accept job offers and tasks only to submit their inability to do the said tasks after a series of failures. This is very true with regards to commitments within families and relationships in general.

3. Recognition

Even though most of the time we fail to acknowledge the office, experience and contributions of other people and give them the respect and support they deserve, we always want our office to be known, our experiences and contributions to be heralded all over the place. This is just the way we humans are. Because of our self-centered nature, we are more inclined to receive from others than to give to them.

Remember that we have said here above that it doesn't take one but two or more people to form a relationship. As Dialogue and Autonomy are important to both the husband and the wife in building the family relationship, so is Recognition. It is always a "give-and-take process." As your spouse recognizes a positive value in you or something important you did for the relationship, it is not time for you to sit on your laurels; you have to reciprocate by also recognizing the positive aspects of your spouse.

First, what do we mean by "recognition?" To recognize someone simply means to acknowledge formally something about that person.

Therefore, in a husband-and-wife relationship, for the husband to recognize his wife means:

1. To acknowledge and respect her status as "wife" as defined by the relationship.

2. Not to withhold or withdraw from her the things which are needed to make her function as a "wife."

3. To appreciate her commitments and protect her status (security).

Let us explain each of these points here-below:

1. Acknowledge Her Engagement Status ("Wife")

First, to *recognize* your wife means to acknowledge her engagement status as your "wife" in the relationship as signed in the marriage certificate. If she is your "wife" in the conjugal relationship, the first thing you should first know about her is that she is a "woman." What this means is that she is not like you, physiologically speaking. Her body isn't built like yours. Her body is weaker than yours. So, you must not let her engage in very tedious tasks within the family or outside of the family, tasks that should be meant for men. If you do, you destroy her body system and she will end up being embittered with you.

As your wife, the woman you marry is supposed to complete you. And she knows this is the reason she is coming into your life and into the relationship. She completes you when she provides a vacuum through which your sperm could be nursed. She completes you when she nurtures the child to grow. She completes you when she keeps your home. She completes you when she keeps you warm. She completes you when she contributes to the decision making process at home. So, when she corrects your faults, for example, please don't scold at her. When you do, she becomes so confused and upset. She asks herself, "Why am I here? Why did he marry me?" This leads her to conclude that you have an ulterior motive for marrying her. And she becomes all the more scared and insecure in the marriage.

As we have said here above, the man and the woman coming together to form a couple is for completion not competition. Completion builds a family. Competition destroys the same. Wives should be particularly careful here. Any attempt to compete with your husband instead of completing him will produce a boomerang effect. That is, it will crush your marriage into pieces.

One way of acknowledging the woman you married as your wife is to recognize that she, too, can contribute into the family decisions even though you, the husband, are the head of the family. You both should operate as a team. That is what the woman knows and expects. As a team, you are pilot and copilot with the same flight manifest. Neither the pilot nor copilot should ignore the warning sign coming from the other. Doing this is heading for a disaster.

2. Do Not Withhold or Withdraw What Makes Her Function

Second, to *recognize* your "wife" means that you should not withhold from her or withdraw from her the things she needs to complete you or the things that make her function as a "woman". What are the things your wife needs to complete you? One of the things a woman needs from her husband is forgiveness. When a man refuses to let go and forgive his wife, he gradually dissociates himself from her emotionally. This opens a loophole in their relationship as the husband may begin daydreaming about being with someone else. Emotionally the relationship is severed, the woman no longer feels being a "wife" complement of the man due to the husband's withholding of forgiveness. The right attitude for spouses should be this: when you love someone, you should look past their imperfections and see the better person they are striving to become.

Another aspect a wife needs to complete her husband is financing. Your wife needs an adequate allowance to take care of your home, especially in case she does not work. Even if she does work, she still needs an allowance from you. This does not have to be much. Note that women, by default, are receivers as men are givers. Receiving makes them happy, especially when it comes from their husband. However, women, too, need to assist their husbands financially.

Lastly, one aspect that you should recognize about women is their ability to talk. When your wife talks to you, please do not shut her up.

When you do, you withdraw from her the thing that makes her a woman – her speech. Even when you have just returned from work, you will recognize that as soon as she sees you she will start charting. That's simply who she is. Even if you are exhausted, it is better you fall asleep while listening to her than tell her you cannot listen to her because you are tired.

3. Appreciate and Protect Your Wife

Why is appreciating your wife very important in the conjugal relationship? It sends an important message that you care and cherish her contributions. This will boost her morale to do even better. When a wife does not get any complement from her husband about her dressing or food, for example, she feels her husband doesn't care about her and the things she does. When she does not get appreciated for her little efforts, she feels she is no longer relevant, and perhaps wanted, in the union (comfort zone of "being recognized" violated). This alone is enough to send her into depression. Gradually, she begins to develop some negative attitudes towards her husband to an extent where she becomes emotionally disconnected from him. And when the wound is not healed, the woman will suddenly find herself out of the union.

Another way of appreciating your wife is to respect and protect her from any danger. The danger may include an assault coming from your parents, friends or your ex-partner. To respect her is to continue to care for her even during times of disagreement. Even in cases when you get gridlocked in your separate positions, you still tell her, "Sweetheart, I love you."

It seems to me that the plight of every wife is "to be recognized" by her husband. And by recognition, we mean the three points we have just mentioned here-above. This is what women see as "true love." No matter how much a husband gives to his wife, no matter how many houses, cars and expensive jewelries he buys for her, the woman would still feel empty inside since she does not have the man's protection. And this will lead to conflict at home even though she may have every other thing.

CHAPTER 4

THE CONFLICT LIFE CYCLE

STAGES OF CONFLICT

Conflict passes through seven successive stages provided no actions are taken to prevent a further escalation. These stages include: (1) *Conflict Potentiality* (2) *Cover-up* (3) *Concession* (4) *Drama* (5) *Precaution* (6) *Rescue* and (7) *No Return*.

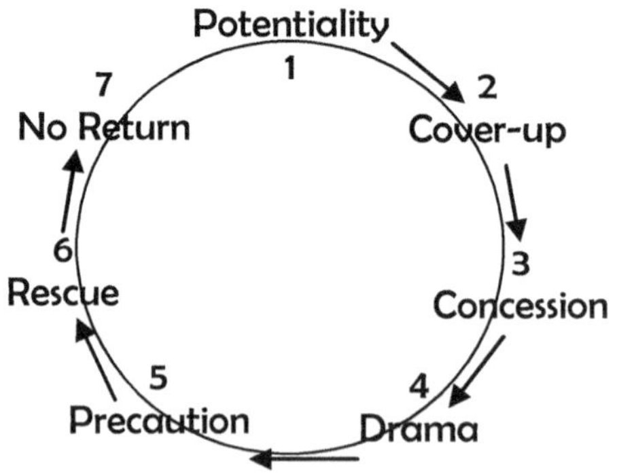

Stage 1:

Conflict Potentiality

Conflict potentiality is the possibility to have an aspect in one's life that upon interaction with another individual may likely cause harm to them or result into an area of disagreement. Note that conflict potentiality is not a probability but a possibility. Because no single human being is ever perfect, every one of us has a conflict potential in us. Note also that because we are self-centered by nature, the conflict potential, what can generate a conflict of interest between us and the people we relate with, can as well be the successes those people have achieved. This is pitiable, but that is just whom we are by nature.

Notwithstanding our conflict potentiality, some people have risen to build good relationships with others. Building a good relationship with family members and friends is only possible when we attempt to pull together the wires of our conflict potential vehemently. This makes it possible for the conflict potential in us to be nearly invisible to others as a threat thereby preparing a good ground for a harmonious relationship with them.

Also, note that conflict potential is not a prejudice. While a prejudice, a preconceived judgment or opinion by one individual about the other, might not necessarily be true, a conflict potential is actually an observable phenomenon in the life of an individual. However, we must also acknowledge here that when negatively reacted upon, prejudices, or prejudgments if you like, can also lead to a conflict in any relationship. However, in this section, we will keep our focus on "conflict potentiality."

The Conflict Potentiality stage marks the beginning of the conflict life cycle. At this stage no tangible conflict can be easily identified between the individuals in relationship. This stage kicks off when two individuals meet for the first time and begin familiarizing themselves with each other and with the demands of the relationship they are intending to build. This usually occurs during the acquaintance and introduction phase of the relationship. Because interaction and communication at this level is usually shallow and superficial, individual preferences, values, beliefs, and goals are yet to be spotted out. However, this first encounter gives both individuals an occasion to anticipate the identity of the other, which would shape the way they view and relate with each other in subsequent meetings. The fact that at this level none of the parties can actually point to a particular phenomenon of future conflict does not mean that such phenomenon does not exist. However, as the relationship continues, gradually they begin to identify aspects in the other that can potentially harm the relationship.

Note that when a conflict potential in one person (carrier) is identified, it can turn into an intrapersonal conflict of the identifier as long as the carrier of the conflict potential remains unaware and the identifier does not express any concerns. The following example will shed more light on this:

> Mike was an enterprising young man who left the city for the village to look for a woman to marry. He was introduced to a beautiful looking woman, Suzy. Mike fell in love with Suzy at first sight and after a while they both made plans to get married. However, there was an aspect in Suzy's life that had always kept Mike bothering since the day they first met. Suzy always spoke more about herself and her family than she spoke about her future marital relations with Mike. This kept Mike wondering back and forth whether this aspect of Suzy's character would engender his marriage life.

When Suzy, the conflict potential carrier, becomes expressly aware of the fact that Mike, the conflict potential identifier, has perceived an aspect of her value or character to be a threat to their relationship, the conflict metamorphoses into stage 2 (Conflict Cover-up) as will be shown here below.

Another example of conflict potentiality could be found in 1 Samuel 18. This had to do with the relationship between King Saul and one of his court men, David. The success of David in defeating Goliath the Philistine generated a conflict potential in David that would sour David's relationship with his master, King Saul. When the women sang praises to the name of David in front of King Saul, it stirred up the king's anger. And from that time onwards King Saul sought ways of assassinating David as shown below (1 Samuel 18:6-8):

When the men were returning home after David had killed the Philistine, the women came out from all the towns of Israel to meet King Saul with singing and dancing, with joyful songs and with timbrels and lyres. As they danced, they sang:

"Saul has slain his thousands, and David his tens of thousands."

Saul was very angry; this refrain displeased him greatly. "They have credited David with tens of thousands," he thought, "but me with only thousands. What more can he get but the kingdom?" And from that time on Saul kept a close eye on David.

Stage 2:
Conflict Cover-up

I begin to speak, but my lips deny passage to my words; a great force sends out my voice, and a greater holds it back. Heavenly gods, you can all witness that this thing that I desire, I do not desire (Seneca, *Phaedra*).

At this stage of the conflict cycle, the conflict potential carrier becomes fully aware of the fact that their counterpart is now aware of their default. However, at this stage, all you have is pretense and cover-up. No one is bold enough to acknowledge their shortcomings. They are afraid of losing their partner or to be seen as the weaker party. Both individuals are still trying to maintain the (false) impression they gave each other when they first met. So, they refrain from talking about their differences hoping that the other party will soon change. At this stage, since their differences are not known to outsiders, they do not feel insecure. So, they continue to carry on with their cover-up lifestyles. However, when their cover-up lifestyles become unbearable, the conflict graduates to the Concession stage.

Even though David was a commander in King Saul's army, the king, covering up his bitterness toward David, hatches a plan to assassinate David, known only to him (the king) as shown below (1 Samuel 18:12-20):

Saul was afraid of David, because the LORD was with David but had departed from Saul. So he sent David away from him and gave him command over a thousand men, and David led the troops in their campaigns. In everything he did he had great success, because the LORD was with him. When Saul saw how successful he was, he was afraid of him. But all Israel and Judah loved David, because he led them in their campaigns.

Saul said to David, "Here is my older daughter Merab. I will give her to you in marriage; only serve me bravely and fight the battles of the LORD." For Saul said to himself, I will not raise a hand against him. Let the Philistines do that!"

But David said to Saul, "Who am I, and what is my family or my clan in Israel, that I should become the king's son-in-law?" So when the time came for Merab, Saul's daughter, to be given to David, she was given in marriage to Adriel of Meholah.

Now Saul's daughter Michal was in love with David, and when they told Saul about it, he was pleased. I will give her to him," he thought, "so that she may be a snare to him and so that the hand of the Philistines may be against him." So Saul said to David, "Now you have a second opportunity to become my son-in-law."

Stage 3:

Conflict Concession

At this stage, one or both parties realize the importance of talking about the issue at hand. So, they begin to seek for ways to end the conflict so as to, at least, hide their shame from the general public. They sit on the table and talk. The offender acknowledges or concedes their misbehavior. However, because concession of misbehavior or wrongdoing does not quench the conflict fire, the offender has no clear intention of discontinuing their misdeed or malpractice. Because they are human, the offender simply regrets the pains they are inflicting upon their counterpart. They think acknowledging their fault and apologizing will at least help to calm down the heat.

Concession of misbehavior and apology gives hope to the offender's counterpart that a true change has come. The victim begins to relate intimately with the offender as before not knowing that the offender was simply staging a show. In a case where the conflict issue is an extramarital affair, the offender would begin to hide or limit their interactions with their concubine or change the places they both used to meet. However, when the victim realizes that they were deceived, the conflict moves to the fourth level, which we call the Drama Stage.

Note that at this stage of conflict, only an insider can be comfortably permitted to intervene in resolving the crisis. By an insider, we mean someone who lives together with one or both parties and has been observing the crisis as it unfolds.

In the case of Saul and David, Saul's son came into David's rescue. Being aware of his father's plot to assassinate David, Jonathan advises his father not to murder David and Saul concedes his fault (1 Samuel 19:4-7):

> Jonathan spoke well of David to Saul his father and said to him, "Let not the king do wrong to his servant David; he has not wronged you, and what he has done has benefited you greatly. He took his life in his hands when he killed the Philistine. The LORD won a great victory for all Israel, and you saw it and were glad. Why then would you do wrong to an innocent man like David by killing him for no reason?"
>
> Saul listened to Jonathan and took this oath: "As surely as the LORD lives, David will not be put to death."
>
> So Jonathan called David and told him the whole conversation. He brought him to Saul, and David was with Saul as before.

Even though Saul's relationship with David returned as it seemed before, this new relationship was simply a make-up on the part of King Saul since the conflict fire was still aflame in the king's heart as we will soon discover. Until the fire of conflict is completely quenched, no true relationship is ever possible.

Stage 4:
Conflict Drama

This is the most delicate stage of any conflict as it breeds injuries to either or both parties in conflict. At this stage, the victim is entirely fed up with the offender's misbehavior and begins to react by throwing insults at the offender, holding the offender for a fight or destroying the offender's belongings. The conflict has now become known to outsiders. Note that the victim's reaction is an act of desperation. They do not want to lose the offender; they simply want them to change. They still cherish them in the relationship. In some cases, the offender continues to harass the victim like the case of Saul as shown below.

David now thinks the mediation of Jonathan has restored his relationship with his master Saul. However, David's new conquest proved him wrong as Saul drives a spear towards him (1 Samuel 19:8-17):

Once more war broke out, and David went out and fought the Philistines. He struck them with such force that they fled before him.

But an evil spirit from the LORD came on Saul as he was sitting in his house with his spear in his hand. While David was playing the lyre, Saul tried to pin him to the wall with his spear, but David eluded him as Saul drove the spear into the wall. That night David made good his escape.

Saul sent men to David's house to watch it and to kill him in the morning. But Michal, David's wife, warned him, "If you don't run for your life tonight, tomorrow you'll be killed." So Michal let David down through a window, and he fled and escaped. Then Michal took an idol and laid it on the bed, covering it with a garment and putting some goats' hair at the head.

When Saul sent the men to capture David, Michal said, "He is ill."

Then Saul sent the men back to see David and told them, "Bring him up to me in his bed so that I may kill him." But when the men entered, there was the idol in the bed, and at the head was some goats' hair.

Saul said to Michal, "Why did you deceive me like this and send my enemy away so that he escaped?"

Stage 5:

Conflict Precaution

After a series of failed attempts to have the conflict fire quenched, the victim systematically withdraws themselves from the offender. The victim also slows down their commitments as they think this might be the best strategy to have the offender change their attitude. Note that at this stage the victim still cherishes the offender and the union in spite of the offender's misbehavior, but at the same time they are scared of what the offender might do to them. The victim now begins to lose hope in the relationship, but feels there is still a 50% chance of saving the relationship. The victim first informs their closed associates like parents, siblings, in-laws, a trusted relative or friend. Note that in case a successful reconciliation takes place, the victim, albeit still being skeptical, may relax the tension a little bit while observing the attitude of the offender.

When reconciliation proves futile, the victim consults a respected authority that can bring peace in the situation. When the peace talk fails, the conflict moves into another stage where the victim requests help from whomsoever, the Conflict Rescue stage.

As a precautionary measure to save his relationship with the king, David runs to the much-respected Prophet Samuel and reports Saul's misbehavior to the prophet, the man who had anointed King Saul and whom the king honors. David did this so that the prophet would caution the king and restore their relationship (1 Samuel 19:18):

> When David had fled and made his escape, he went to Samuel at
> Ramah and told him all that Saul had done to him. Then he and

Samuel went to Naioth and stayed there.

But instead of going to meet the king and find out why he was pursuing David in order to restore David's relationship with the king, the prophet took David to a secluded place, Naioth, where he thought Saul couldn't find David. This was not what David was looking for. Remember that David was a warrior who knew better than the prophet all the places he could hide that King Saul could not find him. David wasn't looking for a hide-out; he was looking for a restoration of his relationship with the king. Because the prophet couldn't salvage David's relationship with the king, David became helpless seeking mediation from whomsoever as we will find in the next stage of conflict.

Stage 6:

Conflict Rescue

At this stage the victim is practically convinced that all their efforts, coupled with the efforts of persons they trusted would have brought a cease-fire, have failed. So, they inform anybody who can be of help requesting them for an immediate intervention. At this level, the deadlock has turned into an SOS exigency. When the offender continues in their misbehavior, the victim finalizes their decision to quit. The conflict graduates into its final stage, the No Return Stage.

After Samuel the prophet had failed in restoring David's relationship with the king, David now runs to his last hope, Jonathan, Saul's own son who loves David as his own biological brother. He complains to Jonathan (1 Samuel 20:1-9):

> Then David fled from Naioth at Ramah and went to Jonathan and asked, "What have I done? What is my crime? How have I wronged your father, that he is trying to kill me?"

> "Never!" Jonathan replied. "You are not going to die! Look, my father doesn't do anything, great or small, without letting me know. Why would he hide this from me? It isn't so!"

> But David took an oath and said, "Your father knows very well that I have found favor in your eyes, and he has said to himself, 'Jonathan must not know this or he will be grieved.' Yet as surely as the LORD lives and as you live, there is only a step between me and death."

> Jonathan said to David, "Whatever you want me to do, I'll do for you."

> So David said, "Look, tomorrow is the New Moon feast, and I am supposed to dine with the king; but let me go and hide in the field until the evening of the day after tomorrow. If your father misses me at all, tell him, 'David earnestly asked my permission to hurry to Bethlehem, his hometown, because an annual sacrifice is being made there for his whole clan.' If he says, 'Very well,' then your servant is safe. But if he loses his temper, you can be sure that he is determined to harm me. As for you, show kindness to your servant, for you have brought him into a covenant with you before the LORD. If I am guilty, then kill me yourself! Why hand me over to your father?"

"Never!" Jonathan said. "If I had the least inkling that my father was determined to harm you, wouldn't I tell you?"

Note that the fact that David had to complain to the king's own son about the atrocities of the king shows how David still cherished his relationship with the king. However, as King Saul did not turn away from his plan to assassinate David, David finally made up his mind to cut off from Saul completely as will be shown in the last stage of the conflict life cycle here-below.

Stage 7:

Conflict No Return

At this stage, the victim is totally convinced there is no way out. They are calm on the outside but inside they are being consumed by the conflict fire. Some husbands who find themselves in this situation might take their wife's external calmness as a sign that she has resolved to succumb to whatever the husband does not knowing that it is instead the worst stage in the conflict life cycle. She makes her plans without consulting anybody for she does not want to be stopped. For her, the only possible solution to escape from the conflict fire is to exit the relationship. When her plans have been concluded, she suddenly quits the relationship never to return.

David, having come into terms with the reality of his relationship with King Saul, decides to abandon the king's court and the activities he does for the king to run away for his dear life (1 Samuel 20:24-29):

> So David hid in the field, and when the New Moon feast came, the king sat down to eat. He sat in his customary place by the wall, opposite Jonathan, and Abner sat next to Saul, but David's place was empty. Saul said nothing that day, for he thought, "Something must have happened to David to make him ceremonially unclean—surely he is unclean." But the next day, the second day of the month, David's place was empty again. Then Saul said to his son Jonathan, "Why hasn't the son of Jesse come to the meal, either yesterday or today?"
>
> Jonathan answered, "David earnestly asked me for permission to go to Bethlehem. He said, 'Let me go, because our family is observing a sacrifice in the town and my brother has ordered me to be there. If I have found favor in your eyes, let me get away to see my brothers.' That is why he has not come to the king's table."

For the first time, and twice in a roll, David was not present at the king's feast. The king was bothered and looked for David, but David was nowhere to be found. From that day onwards, David ran away from Saul until the death of Saul in a fierce battle.

Perhaps, if Saul had not soiled his relationship with David the warrior, the one who defeated the mighty Goliath with just a sling and five pieces of stones would have championed the battle for the king and would have probably rescued the king's life as he did rescue the lives of the entire people of Israel through the defeat of the Philistine giant, Goliath. That was just the price Saul had to pay for his selfish-driven acts toward the innocent David. And there seems to be a price to be paid by every offender of conflict if they do not genuinely repent and change their ways.

CHAPTER 5

CAUSES & EFFECTS OF CONFLICT

A. CAUSES OF CONFLICT

My experience in dealing with all kinds of organizations; big and small, public and private, and for profit and nonprofit, leads me to believe that, more and more, organizations are in the conflict business - not by choice, but certainly to the detriment of almost everything else they are trying to accomplish (Cowan, 2003:4)

Below are some of the major reasons why conflicts have gained too much access and resistance into our families, relationships and the society at large.

1. Conflict Illiteracy

The question to ponder is, "Why has conflict gained too much roots and resistance into many families and relationships today?" Why do we still struggle with how to handle or address any sort of conflict? This social plague is not just living in our families and relationships but it has also permeated every sector of our society, destabilizing or destroying it altogether. Conflict has transformed our marriages into divorces; our parliaments into boxing rings; bilateral relationships between countries into cold wars; friendships into enmities; our peaceful streets into arenas of mass protests; productivity in organizations into non-productivity; employment into unemployment; to name these few.

The answer to the above question is given by Mark Gerzon: *a very large proportion of our generation is conflict illiterate* (Gerzon, 2006:227). In our schools we are taught how to take care of the environment, how to be a good citizen, how to keep fit to maintain a healthy life, but we are never taught how to handle conflict situations. Rare to find in our universities, Gerzon argues, are courses on conflict and negotiation. These courses, if taught, are only offered as extracurricular modules, Gerzon added. So, "many students learn nothing about communicating across differences. If they do, it is often in a 'debate club,' which reinforces the pro/con, either/or way of experiencing differences (Gerzon, 2006:227)." The individual abilities of workers to successfully resolve conflict, David Cowan argues, has a direct link to the quality of conflict management at the organizational level

(Cowan, 2003:25). But how can two people in a relationship manage an issue of conflict when they got no tools in their hands?

> In today's organizations, it is not enough to have job-related skills. It has become vitally important for people to acquire the skills necessary to successfully interact with others and to positively influence organizational culture. Too often we assume employees already possess these skills when, in fact, they don't (Cowan, 2003:6).

2. Worldview Intolerance

Another important reason for the increase in conflicts within relationships is the problem of intolerance of the belief system of each individual involved in the relationship. No one is born into this world with a specific worldview; rather each one of us is taught, either formally or otherwise, how to perceive other people who don't look like us, and how to interpret the things and concepts of this world. And one of the very first institutions where we get such education is religion. For simplicity, we will consider the three major world religions.

In Judaism, people are taught a worldview from a strictly Jewish perspective that is based on the Torah. In Christianity, the Christians are taught the Christian worldview based on the Holy Bible. In Islam, the Muslims are groomed to see the world exclusively through the pages of their sacred Koran. In cases of religious extremism, the

Muslims see the Christians as infidels. The reverse is true. In addition, even members practicing the same religion are further divided by beliefs, race, region, tribe, culture, and language, parameters that have, to a greater extent, limited their scope of action towards outsiders.

> What are we but sedition? like this poor France, faction against faction, within ourselves, every piece playing every moment its own game, with as much difference between us and ourselves as between ourselves and others. Whoever will look narrowly into his own bosom will hardly find himself twice in the same condition. I give to myself sometimes one face and sometimes another, according to the side I turn to. I have nothing to say of myself, entirely and without qualification (Montaigne, in Walter Pater, *Gaston de Latour*).

Thus, there is a very high conflict potential, *a conflict of worldviews*, which already exists among members of the above-mentioned groups. So, when the people who practice the above-mentioned religions become members of the same system, it becomes highly probable that they would react harshly and profusely to any sort of conflict that threatens their ideological stand. As mentioned above, because they are unable to deal with this precarious situation due to conflict illiteracy, the crisis will persist and develop further. The result is an internal unrest and a slow-down or boycott of commitment. This calls for an urgent intervention. To add, when a conflict erupts unexpectedly, the victim does not have the time to consult a book that teaches the steps to take to quench the conflict fire.

As the society becomes more and more globalized with the Americans, Japanese, Australians, Italians, Sri Lankans, Bangladeshis, Kenyans, you name the rest, coming together to work as a team in their organization of employment, and with other third party organizations, the probability of relationships being formed among these people having quite different socio-cultural backgrounds seems very high. The same is true for conflicts in marriages.

3. The Human Pride

It is no more big news that the fundamental problem we humans face today is self-pride. We want to correct others but we do not want to be corrected. Even though we, too, are to take orders, yet we only want to give orders; even though we, too, are to be led; yet we only want to lead. Even though we are less knowledgeable on certain aspects of the family system, we still wear the "know it all" mentality. We claim and affirm we understand who our spouse is and what marriage and the family are all about when in reality we do not. However, we seek the recognition, approval and praises of others even from things we do not deserve much praises. This is the human pride, a force in man that sets up itself as the supreme with regards to wisdom, knowledge, beauty, race, kindness, generosity, courage, dynamism, diligence, prudence, exuberance, faithfulness, gentleness, impartiality, modesty, patience, discipline, sincerity, and you name the rest. This pride sets the person concerned high above others on the pedestal of fantasy. Thus, any action from others such as correction or rebuke may be perceived by the proud as a measure to bring them under subjection. As a way of defense, such action would immediately be met with an objection irrespective of the manner in which the correction or rebuke was made.

The human pride was identified by the 4th/5th century theologian, St. Augustine of Rome, as the major problem that is responsible for the fall and decay of the human race. This position, known as the Augustinian tradition, holds that because we chose not to obey our Creator, we make ourselves the center of our existence:

> Ignoring our Creator, we egocentrically attempt to control reality. We think more highly of ourselves than is warranted. From this angle, grandiosity is the self's nagging tendency. Conceit and arrogance are natural outgrowths of not realizing our limitations in relationship to our Source as well as others (Cooper, 2003:7).

4. The Human Idols

Francis Bacon, the prominent English philosopher of the 16th/17th century, considered one of the greatest thinkers the world has ever had, uses the symbolism of the 'Idols' or 'Illusions' to describe the fundamental defaults in men and in their relations with others, which lead men to poor judgment of events thereby giving rise to chaos. These are the deep-seated causes of human misconception and irrationality. In his famous book, *The New Organon (Novum Organum,* in

Latin), Bacon enumerates four idols that interfere with the processes of clear human reasoning and judgment. These include: *Idols of the Tribe, Idols of the Cave, Idols of the Marketplace,* and *Idols of the Theatre* (Bacon, 2000: XIX).

i) Idols of the Tribe (*Idola tribus*)

These are delusions or illusions or, simply put, false impressions that are embedded in the very human nature. These idols are associated with the specific race, gender, region, social class, etc., to which men identify themselves. These idols have been shaped from history by the men and women of each tribe and have been passed from one generation to another, which has become the norm for sense perception and common practice for all members belonging to that tribe.

> Such then are the idols which I call *Idols of the Tribe,* and which take their rise either from the homogeneity of the substance of the human spirit, or from its preoccupation, or from its narrowness, or from its restless motion, or from an infusion of the affections, or from the incompetency of the senses, or from the mode of impression (Bacon, *The new Organon,* LII).

ii) Idols of the Cave (*Idola specus*)

Unlike *Idols of the Tribe, Idols of the Cave* are illusions that are traceable to a particular individual and which hinder that individual's objective assessment of life issues. Within each tribe every individual has their own specific cave or den, which scatters and discolors the light of nature. These illusions come about as a result of the person's individual nature and as a result of their unique experiences obtained from daily life. A worker who has been racially victimized in the past on several occasions would find it difficult to work amicably with a co-worker of the opposite race. Tensions would be high and the probability of conflict emersion would likewise be high. This is due to the existence of the idols of prejudice in the said worker's cave, which impair them from an objective assessment of the present circumstance.

> The *Idols of the Cave* take their rise in the peculiar constitution, mental or bodily, of each individual; and also in education, habit and accident. Of this kind there is a great number and variety. But I will instance those, the pointing out of which contains the most important caution, and which have most effect in disturbing the clearness of the understanding.... There are found some minds given to an extreme admiration of antiquity, others to an extreme love and appetite for novelty; but few so duly tempered that they can hold the mean, neither carping at what has been well laid down by the ancients, nor despising what is well introduced by the moderns (Bacon, *The new Organon*, LIII-LVI).

iii) Idols of the Marketplace (*Idola fori*)

These are idols that are formed as men engage with one another either for common or unrelated goals. Men interact through the medium of conversation. But the conversation itself is simply an embodiment of words that are applied according to the capacity of the parties in conversation. The intelligence and capacity of the understanding and usage of conversation words of one party may be higher than the other party who may accuse the former of wrongdoings due to the latter's idols of the marketplace – inability to grasp the meaning of words. Because we humans reason through the meanings of words, Bacon affirms, this can be dangerous when the received words are given a false interpretation. This idol, Bacon identifies as the most problematic of all.

> But the *Idols of the Market Place* are the most troublesome of all – idols which have crept into the understanding through the alliances of words and names. For men believe that their reason govern words; but it is also true that words react on the understanding; and this it is that has rendered philosophy and the sciences sophistical and inactive (Bacon, *The new Organon*, LIX).

iv) Idols of the Theatre (*Idola theatri*)

These are illusive knowledge obtained from the books we read and from the plays and movies we watch. These create in our minds a counterfeit world, a world of fantasy, and have the power to misguide our souls to perform acts that are either barbaric or not common among men. The dogmas of religion fall under this category.

But the *Idols of the Theatre* are not innate, nor do they steal into the understanding secretly, but are plainly impressed and received into the mind from the playbooks of philosophical systems and the perverted rules of demonstration…. *Idols of the Theatre* or *of Systems*, are many, and there can be and perhaps will be yet many more. For were it not that now for many ages men's minds have been busied with religion and theology; and were it not that civil governments, especially monarchies, have been averse to such novelties, even in matters speculative; so that men labor therein to the peril and harming of their fortunes – not only unrewarded, but exposed also to contempt and envy – doubtless there would have arisen many other philosophical sects like those which in great variety flourished once among the Greeks. For as on the phenomena of the heavens many hypotheses may be constructed, so likewise (and more also) many various dogmas may be set up and established on the phenomena of philosophy (Bacon, *The new Organon*, LXI-LXII).

5. Negligence

More good intentions, well-conceived programs, personal and organizational vitality, and potentially productive careers lie dead on the road because of poorly managed conflict and its potentially hideous consequences than due to any other ill facing organizations today (Cowan, 2003:4).

From a legal perspective, *negligence* is generally defined as *the failure to exercise reasonable care in a situation that causes harm to others or their property* (Buckley & Okrent, 2004:18). Note that *reasonable care* here is the yardstick that is used for justifying whether an action constitutes negligence or not. And this reasonable care we are talking about is case-specific; that is, it depends largely upon the exact circumstances that surround each case. This phenomenon is described in legal jargon as the "shifting sands" aspect of negligence, an issue legal practitioners often struggle with (Buckley & Okrent, 2004:18-9). Also note that negligence can be either an *act* or *omission*. It is an act or omission when a tortfeasor or caregiver behaves unreasonably by doing a specific careless activity (*negligent* act) or by failing to do something that should have been done to prevent a disaster, i.e., *negligent omission* (Buckley & Okrent, 2004:19).

B. EFFECTS OF CONFLICT

Conflict has the following effects in a family or relationship:

1. Creates a Tensed and Unsafe Environment

Most people go to work expecting to be able to carry out their workplace assignments in an atmosphere which is conducive to effective performance and which is psychologically and emotionally safe. Sadly, as the incidents of workplace bullying increase, so does the degree to which the workplace becomes an unsafe place for the people who are bullied and for those who observe what is happening and worry that they might be next in line (Oade, 2009:1).

As conflict within a family increases, so does the insecurity of members of that family. My experience as a business administrator seems to reveal that a serene working atmosphere constitutes one of the most important factors that foster growth.

No matter how high an organization pays its workers, if the working environment of that organization is tensed, that is, if workers are at constant strives with one another due to management's inefficiency in designing the work to be done or negligence in handling workers' disputes, that organization will eventually suffer a massive loss; loss in productivity (due to the low performance of its workers), loss of manpower/talent (as disappointed, depressed, and heavy-hearted workers quit), and lastly, loss of resources (as it engages more resources - moral, financial, technical, time - to recruit new talents). The same is true with the family set-up. No matter how much a husband caters for the needs of his wife and family, if the family environment is not conducive, the wife and other family members will always feel uncomfortable within the family unit.

2. Self-Isolation

The spouse or family member who has been criticized for their failed attempt to bring a positive change becomes even more cautious and reluctant to fully commit themselves for fear of any further criticisms. As a result, the member gradually isolates themselves from the other members of the system. Such an action, however, leads even to a further criticism by fellow members of the union. The isolated member is accused by others for breaking away from the spirit of the union. Little do the accusers know that they are the victims of the isolation of the one they are accusing due to their improper behavior. The bottom line is that the union as a whole suffers greatly due to the loss in the commitment fraction of the self-isolated member.

3. Destabilizes the Parent-Child Relations

In 1995, a research was carried out by Erel and Burman to investigate the impact marital conflict plays on the parent-child relations, a concept known as the *conflict spillover hypothesis*. This hypothesis holds that negative marital relations give rise to negative parent-child relations as the conflict spills over to the parent-child relationship. On the contrary, positive marital relations will give rise to positive parent-child relations thanks to the absence of marital conflict (Turner & West, 2015: 95).

In 2002, a similar research was carried out by Buehler and Gerard.

The findings reveal that parental involvement in the parent-child relationship decreases as marital conflict increases. Parents who are affected by conflict have less time to be attentive to their children. Some parents go as far as drawing their children into the middle of the marital conflict (Turner & West, 2015: 95).

As shown by the above findings, most often, it is the innocent children who fall victims of the misunderstandings that their parents go through. Instead of seeking ways of settling their disputes, parents in dispute seem not to find it embarrassing to include their children into the mess they themselves created.

In some cases, the prevailing conflict may push a parent to relate with their children as if the children were adults or their peers. They begin to reveal sensitive information about their partner to their children with the intention of damaging their partner's character, which ends up destroying the said partner's relationship with their children as well. This concept is known in the social sciences as *Triangulation*, a phenomenon scholars consider as a boundary regulation problem in the family system (Turner & West, 2015: 96).

4. Leads to Waste of Resources

When we examine the negative results of poorly managed or unmanaged conflict, we see resources squandered on unproductive, if not counterproductive activities. On the other hand, when conflict is well managed and dealt with effectively, we not only conserve resources, we produce them (Cowan, 2003:9)

One of the results of a poorly arbitrated conflict is that it leaves the unsatisfied party wounded. As a result, the latter engages in actions that only undermine the success of the union. Such actions may range from the abuse of other members of the union like the children through the misuse of resources belonging to the union to the willful commission of acts that delegitimize the relationship such as one or both spouses seeking for an extra-marital affair. Note that all these actions are done as a means of hurting the other party to provoke them come to the dialogue table for resolution.

5. Drains Your Investments

Conflict drains the investments that have been made over the years in a marriage, relationship or business. The reason your business may be going down is not because of the economic or political climate of the place where the business is situated. Granted, your business could be affected by the aforementioned factors. However, the down trend of your business is a direct consequence of the prevailing conflicts in your family and relationships. The health of your family interactions and relationships plays an important role in the health of your business. The fire that comes out of a conflict does not get stuck in the system; this fire moves out of the system and spreads itself all over the investments and associations of the system member. Until the fire is quenched, do not expect any return to normalcy in your business.

Please, note that conflict is not just physical; it is as well a spiritual entity. There is a connection between the physical and the spiritual. The spiritual aspect of any phenomenon is the root of that phenomenon. Meanwhile its physical component is simply the manifestation of the spiritual reality – the aspect we can see, hear, touch and smell. Therefore, to restore sanity into your investments, the fire of conflict in your family must be quenched by addressing the root causes of the conflict.

6. Loss of Trust in the Partner and Union

As the body shelters the soul, so should the husband, who is, by default, the head of the family union, protect and guard his wife and children from any possible threat that may emanate from within or without the walls of their family unit.

> People who have been bullied, or who are currently being bullied, often feel betrayed by their employing organization. They find it inexcusable that senior managers who know about the issues they are facing can fail to confront the bullies and require them to stop using abusive behavior in the workplace (Oade, 2009:1).

The trust members of a family or relationship have in the family head or leadership is indispensable. Once this trust is lost, disorder and chaos within the family or relationship will follow. Imagine a scenario in a gathering where a woman who initially had an affair with a man begins to publicly harass the man's wife. Instead of the man defending his wife by coming to her rescue, he pleads with his wife to ignore his ex-partner while, at the same time, avoiding to confront the latter. No woman on earth will feel secure to have such a man by her side as a husband. The man's action toward his legitimate wife sends a strong message to her as to whom his preference lies.

7. Causes Depression, Illness or Death

Conflict has a great potential of inciting psychological or physical pain in its victims, which may ultimately have grievous consequences. This claim, I strongly believe is not difficult to grasp especially if you are or have been in any relationship of conflict crisis. Concerning the above fact, Knapp & Daly write,

> Although conflict has the potential to increase understanding, stimulate positive change, and facilitate human relations, all too often conflict leads to intolerance and physical and psychological harm. The dysfunctional consequences of conflict are evident in terrorist activities and warfare between groups and nations, but they are not confined to interactions between members of such macroentities (Knapp & Daly, 2002:475).

Scientific facts reveal the following physical and psychological harm conflict inflicts upon its victims (Colbert, 2003:9-10).

- In a ten-year study, individuals who could not manage their emotional stress had a 40% higher death rate than non-stressed individuals.

- A Harvard Medical school study of 1,623 heart-attack survivors concluded that anger brought on by emotional conflicts doubled the risk of subsequent heart attacks compared to those who remained calm.

- A heart disease study at the Mayo Clinic found that psychological stress was the strongest predictor of future cardiac events, including cardiac death, cardiac arrest, and heart attack.

8. Affects Outsiders and Reignites the Conflict Fire

Conflict in a family affects not only members of its household, who are directly involved, it also affects those who are indirectly involved like in-laws and friends.

When a husband and wife have an unresolved issue, outsiders, who normally take sides, may be affected by the prevailing situation. An outsider who will normally favor a party of their interest will act in ways that may reignite the conflict fire afresh. By default, the husband's parents, for instance, will stand with their son irrespective of the logic of argument in force. The reverse is true with the wife's parents.

9. Other Effects

According to Rahim (2001:7), conflict has the following disadvantages both to a union and its members:

- Conflict may cause stress, burnout, and dissatisfaction.

- Communication between individuals and groups may be reduced.

- Relationships may be damaged.

- A climate of distrust and suspicion can be developed.

- Commitment and loyalty may be affected.

- Resistance to change can increase.

CHAPTER 6

QUENCHING
THE CONFLICT FIRE
&
ITS BENEFITS

Note Carefully the Following Three Points:

1. Focus on Root Causes, Not on Symptoms

The best way to resolve a conflict is to quench the conflict fire completely. To quench the fire, you must focus on the conflict itself. This will keep you away from aberrations and bias. When all factors of the conflict are dealt with, other things will automatically take shape. This, I would suggest, should be the goal and approach of anyone who undertakes the charge of resolving conflict issues between friends, couples or family members. So, we must not just focus on uniting people together without completely taking out the plague that put them apart in the first place. We must beware of performing a cosmetic surgery type of conflict resolution. I have seen a few cases of poorly managed conflicts where couples even embraced each other only to be separated on the same issue. They were given some false hopes of living together again after a few issues were identified. But because some other pertinent concerns were left unidentified, the fire picked up and its flame grew and kept burning at an even larger proportion.

I don't know if you reading this book are a Christian or not, but there is a story in the Christian Bible that is worth mentioning here. This story is recorded in Matthew 12:43-45 where it is said that when an unclean spirit is cast out of a person, it goes around looking for whom to possess. When that spirit finds no available human vessel, it will go verify the body from which it came out to see if it is empty. When the spirit discovers that its former vessel of abode is empty, it will not possess it straightaway but will go and look for seven other unclean spirits that are more wicked than itself and together they will come and possess the empty body making it difficult for the eight spirits to be cast out altogether.

True conflict resolution involves addressing <u>all</u>, not some, root causes. When we do not address all the root causes of conflict, the scenario may turn out to be like that of the man above who became possessed by eight wicked unclean spirits, which made his case even worse than before.

A prolific writer on social conflict to mention here is De Borno (1986). For De Borno, to resolve a conflict means to eliminate the conflict entirely. De Borno coined the terms "confliction" meaning "to create conflict" and "de-confliction" meaning "to eliminate conflict." De-confliction does not refer to negotiation or bargaining or even to the resolution of conflicts. De-confliction is the effort required to evaporate a conflict. Just as confliction is the setting up of a conflict, so de-confliction is the opposite process: the demolition of the conflict (De Borno, 1986: 5).

2. Intervene Timely & Specifically

When the kitchen section of an apartment building is on fire, to prevent the fire from spreading across the apartment rooms, all efforts must be directed towards the kitchen room that is ablaze, to extinguish it, and bring it under control. The same is true for strives, scuffles, combats, and disputes that occur within the family unit and relationships. Like the fire in the kitchen room, conflict between any two members of a family must be extinguished immediately to prevent it from spreading further into the entire family unit.

Note that conflict is like cancer. If care is not taken, the cancer that develops in a man's foot, for example, may spread to other parts of his body. Preventing the conflict spill-over requires a family leadership that puts its members first, a leadership that assumes the great responsibility of cleaning its house to increase the potential of commitment and collaboration among members.

3. The Approach Taken Will Determine the Result

Conflict resolution is a task that must be given proper attention. It must neither be postponed nor ignored. Conflict resolution must be timely, appropriate, and unbiased. No one resolution method applies to all cases of conflicts. The method to be applied depends largely upon the nature of the conflict. Note that not all resolved conflicts lead to the same result. The quality of change that is experienced by the affected parties of conflict following a resolution depends largely upon the negotiating skills that were employed in the resolution process.

PREREQUISITES FOR QUENCHING THE CONFLICT FIRE

1. Be Optimistic & Goal-oriented

In the famous story of the three bricklayers working side by side, each of them is asked, "What are you doing?" One replies, "I am laying bricks." The second replies, "I am constructing a wall," but the third answered, "I am building a cathedral." While the first two bricklayers had a narrow scope of the project by limiting their vision, the third carried the vision all along. While the other workmen were process-oriented, the third was goal-oriented. While they saw the building of a cathedral as an ambiguous task, the third saw the building process already completed in the construction of the wall.

The same applies to a family member or outsider who launches an enquiry to resolve a family-related conflict. Some negotiators may boycott the resolution process during the investigation phase after having observed the complex nature of the conflict in question.

Note that,

> A workable rule of thumb holds that the consequences of an unmanaged or poorly managed conflict are disproportionately larger than the conflict itself. We should keep this rule in mind when we are tempted to dismiss a conflict because we don't think it requires our attention. Nowhere in life is the adage "an ounce of prevention is worth a pound of cure" more applicable than in the realm of conflict (Cowan, 2003:29).

To appease themselves that they have at least done something, the negotiator comes up with measures that do not really deal with the root cause of the problem. Such negotiators are short-sighted. They are like the two bricklayers with the narrow vision mentioned here above. They are intimidated by the complexity of the conflict fire. They fail to see what benefits the family stands to gain when the conflict fire is entirely extinguished.

In a marriage setting, intimidated by the consequences of her action, a wife chooses not to talk to her husband about his unfaithfulness or abuse of their children or property. She forgets to understand that not talking about these things only gives her husband a leeway to continue in his misbehaviors, which will cause even more disaster in their union. Because of the fear of the unknown, this woman chooses to die silently. She lacks optimism in conflict resolution. If you are the one reading this book, wake up my dear sister. Your passiveness will not bring back your joy. You have to be proactive to restore what you are about to lose or what you have already lost, if that be the case. In doing this, remember this: Target the root cause of conflict, not the person. Your redemptive action will inspire your spouse of the great woman in you, and this will build your relationship even stronger than before. I see you on the top.

When asked about the challenges he faces in managing organizational crisis, Mark Swilling, co-director of the Sustainability Institute, said, "The leadership challenge, from our point of view, is not to get discouraged by the logic of the existing system. The leadership challenge that excites me is to inspire the system to change" (Gerzon, 2006:219). A non-change in the attitude of family members reveals the prevalence of conflict. A true resolution of conflict brings genuine system change: restores order and boosts commitment.

2. Empathy

A well-known American is known to have said, "We should not judge another person until we have walked two moons in his moccasins." The implication here is that we should always try to envisage or imagine how a person in conflict feels before we can make any judgment. In other words, we should walk in the moccasins of the person in conflict for a while as this would enable us make an objective assessment of what they are going through.

Empathy, as defined by Avery, is "the ability to recognize and understand another person's perceptions and feelings, and to accurately convey that understanding through an accepting response" (Samovar et al., 2010:389). Talking about empathy from a cultural perspective, Ting-Toomey writes, "Through empathy we are willing to imaginatively place ourselves in the dissimilar other's cultural world and to experience what she or he is experiencing" (Samovar et al., 2010: 389). As important as cultural values are, we must stress that more emphasis must be placed on the psychological state of the persons at conflict. To this, Miller & Steinberg remark, "To communicate interpersonally, one must leave the cultural and sociological levels of predications and physically travel to the psychological level" (Samovar et al., 2010:389).

Note that empathy is a complex activity composed of many variables as Bell describes here bellow:

Cognitively, the empathic person takes the perspective of another person, and in so doing strives to see the world from the other's point of view. Affectively, the empathic person experiences the emotions of another; he or she feels the other's experiences. Communicatively, the empathic individual signals understanding and concern through verbal and nonverbal cues (Samovar et al., 2010:389).

In one of the Churches I had worked in the past, a case was reported to our resident pastor. This had to do with a sexual scandal committed by an assistant pastor to my coworker's fiancée who had been sent to the assistant pastor for counseling services. During investigation, it was discovered that the assistant pastor took the opportunity of the absence of his wife (who had travelled to visit her parents) and invited the victim over to their matrimonial residence where the twenty-year-old victim was sexually abused.

After the victim had reported the matter to the resident pastor and the claim established to be true, the resident pastor, as a way of resolving the crisis, called my coworker into his office and apologized for what went wrong, and (shockingly) said, "Please, don't let the Church members know about this for it will damage the reputation of our Church." When I heard about that, I was boiling inside me not just for the resident pastor's attempt to cover up the abuse but for the fact that no punitive sanctions were given to the culprit. The same culprit came into the office the next day conducting business as usual. He would even come boldly into our office (Accounting & Finance office) to make cash requests. I felt frustrated, battered and tattered on my coworker's behalf each time I saw the culprit walking freely while my coworker and his fiancée were in tremendous pain. For my coworker, business was not as usual. Being my assistant and sharing the same office, I saw how my coworker lost every bit of motivation to work. He could barely balance the books of accounts. His input consistently went down and down until he decided to quit after having secured a job in a secular company.

3. Know Well to Resolve Well

Why is understanding the plight and values of members of a family or relationship so important in leadership and conflict prevention? A great leader, to borrow Hitler's words, is a *Menschenkenner*. That is, "one who grasps - instinctively, intuitively or otherwise - the motives of men" (Hodgkinson, 1991:67).

Over the past 2000 years, emotions have been regarded to occupy a central role in organizational management (Mastenbrock, 2000). Fayol, for example, stressed that leaders should understand so well all aspects of their workers' psyches including their emotional states (Bryman et al., 2011:365).

The heart of a man reveals the things that are going on in that man's life at any given point in time. With regards to the family unit, a member's psyche is the mental duplex of that member, which has been gradually constructed over the years with the ideas and values picked up from the family unit and the society at large. No one can predict how another person really feels unless they engage in a friendly talk with them. In the same way, no individual can know how their counterpart feels about the relationship unless they talk with the latter from time to time. Casual but frank conversations with union members will give birth to shocking revelations about the family practices or moral attitudes that disgruntle members.

Spouses and family members must also be able to understand the feelings of other members of the family irrespective of the latter's attempt to suppress or conceal them from view. Knowing to some extent the different ways through which each family member expresses frustration would be helpful since emotional expression varies with persons. Understanding parameters like facial expressions, gestures, tone of voice, moods, etc., which are used in expressing frustrations would be very critical in launching an investigation that seeks to quench the conflict fire off your family.

4. Be an Effective Communicator

Communication is defined by Lehman & Dufrene as "the process of exchanging information and meaning between or among individuals through a common system of symbols, signs, and behavior" (Lehman & Dufrene, 2010:4). Good communication skills on the part of the negotiator are vital ingredients for quenching the conflict fire. These skills require that the negotiator be attentive and observant as the concerned parties talk, making inferences from and responding logically to each party's arguments. Effective communication does to the soul what medicine does to the body. It heals a broken soul, relieves it from pressure and re-conditions it to a "new state" through the mechanism of persuasion.

Charles Darwin & the Principles of Expression

On the importance of understanding the principles of expression, Charles Darwin in *The Principle of Antithesis* developed in *The Expression of the Emotions in Man and Animals,* considered one of his most scholarly works, writes:

With social animals, the power of intercommunication between the members of the same community, - and with other species, between the opposite sexes, as well as between the young and the old, - is of the highest importance to them. This is generally affected by means of the voice, but it is certain that gestures and expressions are to a certain extent mutually intelligible. Man not only uses inarticulate cries, gestures, and expressions, but has invented articulate language; if, indeed, the word INVENTED can be applied to a process, completed by innumerable steps, half-consciously made. Anyone who has watched monkeys will not doubt that they perfectly understand each other's gestures and expression, and to a large extent, as Rengger asserts, those of man (Darwin, 2007:30).

PROCEDURES FOR QUENCHING THE CONFLICT FIRE

Here is a procedure that should be observed in quenching the conflict fire skillfully and in a way that leaves both parties unhurt and satisfied:

- Talk privately with each party in conflict to have their own side of the story. As each party talks, make sure you listen attentively and take notes. Note that the intention of the speaker is to be heard, to be understood, and to be sympathized with. Also note that no judgment should be based on a one-sided story. The negotiator's aim here is to have a full understanding of what led to the conflict at hand — putting one and one together, i.e., making a joint analysis of the two narratives.

- Invite both parties for a dialogue.

- Acknowledge a difficult situation exists.

- Acknowledge both parties have some reasons for being offended. Let them know that in most cases of conflicts, neither party is right nor wrong; rather, parties' distinctive perceptions collide to form an array of disagreement.

- Share a cup of drink together with both parties to drown anger.

- Share a conflict experience or story to enable parties know that conflicts are quite a natural phenomenon.

- Listen effectively to both parties as they share their story.

Effective listening demands that the listener be calm, dispassionate, and sincere. Make sure you understand so well what each party is saying. If not, ask questions focusing on the party's side of the story. Being passionate can send a bad message to the other party that you are being subjective or biased, which may hamper the whole process of negotiation.

Note that in cases of conflict involving a husband and his wife, one party, usually the wife, may willfully avoid making certain confessions that may damage the reputation of her husband. The wife may feel very uncomfortable to speak up against her husband in the latter's presence for fear of retaliatory sanctions, which, in most cases, come in a disguised fashion. In such a situation, memo previously taken from the one-to-one talk could guide the negotiator, who should be a person much respected by both parties in conflict. At this juncture, the negotiator can remind and request the wife if she would like to restate any omitted claims. However, prior to this exercise, the husband must be kindly cautioned not to take any disguised punitive measures against his wife due to the latter's confessions.

- Establish a common area of agreement, no matter how small, and complement both parties for this.

- Define the area of disagreement.

- Take effective action to resolve the area of disagreement: This is the level that requires enough application of brainpower after a careful and objective analysis of the conflict situation. The quality of decision taken would determine the amount of flames to be extinguished and the quality of liberation experienced by both parties. The negotiator <u>must</u> be careful to avoid slanting for whatsoever reasons.

- Determine what to do such as bringing in a higher authority or an expert in family therapy for mediation if conflict remains unresolved.

Caution to Conflict Negotiators:

Let Your Decision Be Free and Fair

We must caution against taking any decisions that are geared towards satisfying the innocent party. The latter will always want the "worse than the worst" punishment to be given to the defaulter. Even if the innocent party is not happy about the decision of the negotiator, that shouldn't bother the negotiator in any way provided that the negotiator's judgments are perceived to be free and fair, ceteris paribus.

WHAT MUST BE DONE TO PREVENT CONFLICT

1. Eliminate Private Interest

Private or self-interest is one of the greatest causes of conflict in families and relationships. When private interest is eliminated in pursuit of the common goal of the system, conflicts would be at their minimum, if not eliminated.

In *The Republic,* Plato submitted that the needs of every society could be satisfied only when private property is eliminated (Rahim, 2001:2). Thus, when private interests do interplay and the result does not promote or contribute to the accomplishment of the common goal, a conflict is born. Conflict, therefore, does not exist until each member abandons the common goal in pursuit of their personal interests. Thus, the absence of conflict, Plato and Aristotle did stress, is a sine qua non for the achievement of the common goal. For these philosophers, "strife is a sign of imperfection and unhappiness. Order marks the good life and disorder the opposite. Conflict is a threat to the success of the state [family] and should be kept at an absolute minimum, and removed altogether if possible" (Sipka,

1969:7).

The introduction of private interest into a marriage relationship destroys that relationship. This is because marriage, by default, is regarded as the creation of two persons - a man and his wife – and it is only developed from the cumulative efforts and resources of both spouses. To make matters worse, when a couple has signed for a joint-property arrangement, any act of private ownership of business or investment by one party betrays the agreement and grieves the other party. In the case of a joint-property marriage arrangement, any project that each spouse wishes to carry on must be brought to the attention of the other. And both must agree before it could be pursued. The moment you got married, you both ceased being free moral agents, 'free' in the sense of making unilateral decisions.

Note that the husband and his wife are the two shareholders of their marriage. Just like in a shareholding company where no decision could be taken without the consultation of every other shareholder, I do not advise any spouse to make unilateral decisions without consulting their counterpart. Doing this is opening the doors of your family wide open for conflict to strike.

We understand that we all are selfish by nature. We want to do our things without being influenced by anyone including the people we claim to be so united with. But we have to count the cost. No one engages into a venture without first calculating how much it would cost them. Counting the cost should guide all our actions in marriage and relationships.

2. Family Education

"If you think education is expensive, try ignorance."
(Derek Bok, Harvard University President)

One way to prevent family members from the plague of conflict is through education. Both the husband and wife must encourage each other to read books on Marriage and the Family. Together, the husband and wife can also watch movies on the family, highlighting the strengths and weaknesses of those movies and applying the positive aspects in their family. Note that it is not knowledge learned but knowledge applied that brings a change. They should also talk about possible threats to their union and come up with strategies that will prevent those threats from crushing their family whenever they arise. They should also learn to value the contributions of each other and keep the *family secret* from outsiders as much as possible.

A thorough education and training will also help in reducing the amount of supervision on your children and other members of your household. Note that your children can only become the best version of themselves to the extent of your sacrifice in educating them.

What makes your family work is not how rich you are, neither is it how influential you may be in the society. What really makes your family work is *time*. You need to invest adequate time in your family. It takes work to build a good family. You need time to talk with your wife, to listen to her plight, to have a romance with her. You need time to train up your children in the direction of their callings. All these things cannot be done with money. Even if you have someone hired to train your children, they will be imparting their values, not your values, into your children, which may end up destroying your children's future.

What about your spouse? Because you were so busy at work and whenever you return home you simply want to eat and go to bed, would you hire someone to have a romance with your wife on your behalf? I guess the answer is an emphatic "No." Ignoring all these things, which are your first responsibilities, in pursuit of silver and gold is a very unwise decision, one that destroys your home.

Family education must be ongoing. The moment you stop is the moment you and members of your household begin to encounter difficulties in handling social issues, which will ultimately result to the knocking off of heads. According to Plato, "Evil actions are the result of ignorance." When education stops, ignorance creeps in and the result is chaos within the family dynamics. Let's listen to what Harvey Ullman had to say concerning the importance of education:

> "Anyone who stops learning is old, whether this happens at twenty or eighty. Anyone who keeps on learning not only remains

young, but is consistently more valuable regardless of physical capacity."

The more valuable your spouse and children feel they are, the happier they will become. The happier they are, the less troublesome they will be to you as their husband and father.

3. Discipline

Every child needs discipline. Without discipline a child is like a ship with no captain on board. The sinking of such a ship is unstoppable.

Another form of education worthy to mention here is discipline. Most parents feel when they do not discipline their children they are showing them love. They are afraid that when they discipline their child they may lower the child's self-esteem. Let me disappoint you and let me shock you with this: Do you know that each time you fail to discipline your child you are breaking God's law of creation, and when you do the consequences will follow both you (mental stress) and your child (death)?

Now, the Bible emphatically states in Proverbs 23:13-14:

"Do not withhold discipline from a child; if you punish them with the rod, they will not die. Punish them with the rod and save them from death."

As clearly shown above, when you punish your children with the rod they will not die. The reverse is true. That is, when you do not punish your children with the rod they will die. This death can be either spiritual or physical. What this means is that any attempt not to discipline your children is an attempt to kill them. Only God knows how many parents have killed and are still killing their children today through the act of non-discipline. God has entrusted discipline into the hands of parents because He knows no child can survive today in this wicked world without the discipline of their parents.

A man who killed his sons by his failure to discipline them when they went wrong is Eli the priest. Eli's three sons treated the Lord's offering with contempt when they extorted meat offering from the Israelites. They collected raw meat from the people, contrary to the custom of the sacrifice. They even threatened the people that if they failed to hand the raw meat over to them, they would take it by force. This angered the Lord who made a vow to kill them (1 Samuel 3:11-14):

> And the LORD said to Samuel: "See, I am about to do something in Israel that will make the ears of everyone who hears about it tingle. At that time I will carry out against Eli everything I spoke against his family—from beginning to end. For I told him that I would judge his family forever because of the sin he knew about; his sons blasphemed God, and he failed to restrain them. Therefore I swore to the house of Eli, 'The guilt of Eli's house will never be atoned for by sacrifice or offering.'"

Had these young men been properly disciplined by their father the moment their atrocity was brought to their father's notice, they would have stopped their evil practice, which would have saved their lives. Don't let your children to die by refusing to discipline them. It's never too late.

4. Develop the Genius Ability of Your Household

"Natural abilities are like natural plants; they need pruning by study…" (Francis Bacon)

If there is one thing that every member of a family or relationship aspires for, one thing that every married person truly yearns for, that one thing is *skill and career development*. No one wants to remain at the same level of academic knowledge and performance throughout their entire life. Let me borrow the 'Prison and Warden' analogy used by Dr. Sunday Adelaja in his masterpiece, *Church Shift*. Some wives are like prisoners: their home is like a prison and their husbands are like the wardens. They do not want to be confined in the prison home, but they have been forced to. They have no option but to bear the pain of their imprisonment. They are asking themselves this question every day, "When will I be released from this prison?" Therefore, it is incumbent upon the husband to ask his wife what she wants to do, and sponsor her. However, if your wife feels comfortable about her present status, that is fine. The point is that it should be left for her to decide, not you. All you can do as her husband is to guide her choice. Today, many single ladies are busy looking for a man who will not just express love to them by showering them with flowers but who can develop them mentally and spiritually and provide them with security, too.

Another major reason why wives are longing for their career development is that such progress would provide a strong security to them in the marriage. It gives them, too, a voice in the union. They feel they, too, can contribute to the decision-making process. Also, they know that even if their husband fires them through divorce, they will not be stranded and dependent on anyone. With their skills, they can easily find something to do to make a living. Also, when you invest in a sincere wife you make her to be more responsible and more respectful to you, with the exception of a few wives.

The same should apply to your children and other members of your household. Your children have stayed at the same level they are right now not because they wanted to, but because you have not taken the time to encourage and develop them. You must discover their talents and help them grow in them. Note that as the head of the family, your family is a platform God has given you to change men and women, to change the society, to change the nation and to change the world. You are the reformer of your family. This is your divine responsibility. If you fail in this responsibility, you have failed God. A failed family is a failed society, and by extension a failed nation.

5. Be a Father

Permit me remind you of what Albert Einstein, one of the greatest scientists of all time, said, "I am neither especially clever nor especially gifted. I am only very, very curious." As a father, you must be curious about the future of your children. What will my child become in the future? What should I do to help them achieve what they came to do here on earth? These two questions must guide your actions toward your children. Remember that your children are your very seeds (Greek for *sperm*), which you did plant in your wife. As a gardener owes the plants in their garden the responsibility of watering and pruning them for them to grow, you owe your children (your seeds) a great responsibility of caretaking until the time when they become a tree, in which time they can virtually take care of themselves.

Fatherhood is not a one-time event. Fatherhood is a series of events. What makes you a father is not your ability to sow seeds. On the contrary, what makes you a father is your ability to nurture the seeds you sowed. For me, the concept of *a caring father* does not exist. This is because a father is someone who cares for their children in the first place. Fatherhood is not about "what you did once in a lifetime." Fatherhood is about "what you are doing now and will always do." It is gross wickedness to sow a seed and not take care of that seed. This is anticipatory murder. It is the caring process that maintains the life of a seed. To kill a seed all you simply have to do is to stop caring for that seed. Once that is done, the seed will automatically die. I see many who call themselves fathers who are nothing but murderers. They are murderers because they have abandoned the singular thing they are mandated to do to keep their children alive.

If you fall under this category, please wake up. The reason why your children do not have respect for you is because they do not really "feel" and "perceive" you as their father. They do not "feel" you are their father because you have not proven that to them. The only thing they know about you is that you had been simply introduced to them as their father by either their mother or someone else. They have struggled to put one and one together. Some have even forced themselves to believe what they had been told over the years to no avail. As far as they are concerned, you are "a father by information."

As long as you do not take care of your children, the woman who bore those children will find it very difficult to be contented with you. For her, you may ignore her but don't ignore the seeds you once planted in her. She can easily pass over some of the things you did against her, but she will find it very hard to wipe out the fact that you did abandon your own children.

Note that the same is true with respect to wives. As a wife, when you abandon your little children to be nurtured by their father who, by default, has no mother-like experience in bringing up children, you make it very difficult for the man to forget this pain you inflicted upon him and the children – abandoning the care you should have given to your children as a mother.

Most conflicts in families stem from this phenomenon. As a man, if you really want peace in your home, if you really want to be loved and given your place as a husband and father in your home, then you must restore the fatherhood you have lost by undoing your wrongs. Always ask yourself regularly, "Am I a father or a stranger to my children? Do I behave like a father or a tyrant?" As a father, you are to thrust yourself into your family because that's where your primary assignment or calling is. Who you really are is not determined by the kindness you show to outsiders but by your attitude toward your family.

There is a man in the bible that fits the stereotype of a "father." His name is Job. Job so much loved and cared for his children that he was very curious about their state of being whenever they had gone away from him. Job was so curious that he prepared a burnt offering on behalf of his children just in case they had broken the command of God. This custom, Job did regularly. Job was very careful for his children not to come under the wrath of God as we find here below (Job 1:5):

> When a period of feasting had run its course, Job would make arrangements for them to be purified. Early in the morning he would sacrifice a burnt offering for each of them, thinking, "Perhaps my children have sinned and cursed God in their hearts." This was Job's regular custom.

It is your duty to be curious about your children. It may be shocking to know that some parents do not even know where their children go to, whom they hang around with and what they want to become in life. That should not be the case.

As little as children may be, God honors a child because He sees a nation in a child. Do not take your children for granted by ignoring their requests or abandoning them altogether. Abandoning them is refusing them growth. And if you do this, how do you expect God to prosper you? There is a man in the Bible whose name was Onan. Onan was supposed to bring forth children for his late brother, according to their tradition, so that his late brother's name would not be wiped out from history. But during the process of planting the seed into the late brother's wife, Onan spilled it on the floor instead thereby destroying the seed. Because of this act, Onan was destroyed by God. While Onan saw the seed as a minute thing that could be destroyed, God saw the murder of a child (Genesis 38:8-10):

> Then Judah said to Onan, "Sleep with your brother's wife and fulfill your duty to her as a brother-in-law to raise up offspring for your brother." But Onan knew that the child would not be his; so whenever he slept with his brother's wife, he spilled his semen on the ground to keep from providing offspring for his brother. What he did was wicked in the LORD's sight; so the LORD put him to death also.

This passage is not meant to scare you but to bring to your attention how important your children are in the eyes of God. When you do not value them, God will probably not value you. When you reject them, do not expect God's favor. Until you repent and start caring for your children like a father, you may never enjoy true joy in your life and family. It's never too late.

6. Create Rules and Standards

One of the main reasons why conflicts occur in a geometric fashion in most families and relationships today is due to the absence of well-defined rules and standards or the lack of their application in the established union. When rules and standards are no longer in force, some members of the union, including outsiders, take good advantage of this to operate as they so wish – leaving the family home and returning there anytime, hanging around with an outsider without the knowledge and approval of the parents or an elder member of the house or union. These are actions that will only lead to more family crises.

Note that a family is not great by virtue of its wealth. A family is great by the wealth of its virtue. The wealth of a family does not shield that family from the flames of conflict. However, the virtue of a family will. Good virtues will save a family from so many crises. The earlier you create strict rules in your family the better.

One of the failures of the first man, Adam, was that, as the head of the family, Adam did not create a solid Rules and Standard system for his family. So, the enemy seized this opportunity to creep in and poison the mind of his wife. Adam was given a command by God. So, if anyone was to know anything about this command, Adam should have been the one to be contacted first, not his wife. In addition, Adam was the head of the family. So, it was very logical that he should have been the spokesperson. But because Adam did not build a solid structure for rules and standards regarding his family, the enemy took advantage and destroyed his family as we find in Genesis 3:1-6:

> Now the serpent was more crafty than any of the wild animals the LORD God had made. He said to the woman, "Did God really say, 'You must not eat from any tree in the garden'?" The woman said to the serpent, "We may eat fruit from the trees in the garden, but God did say, 'You must not eat fruit from the tree that is in the middle of the garden, and you must not touch it, or you will die.'" "You will not certainly die," the serpent said to the woman. "For God knows that when you eat from it your eyes will be opened, and you will be like God, knowing good and evil."

> When the woman saw that the fruit of the tree was good for food and pleasing to the eye, and also desirable for gaining wisdom, she took some and ate it. She also gave some to her husband, who was with her, and he ate it. Then the eyes of both of them were opened, and they realized they were naked; so they sewed fig leaves together and made coverings for themselves.

Note that after the woman must have eaten the fruit, she gave some to her husband who unquestionably also ate. This shows how loose Adam's home was. It should have been Adam's place as the protector of the family unit to have first known who the serpent really was before accepting anything from the latter. Secondly, note that the serpent did question the integrity of the command that was given to Adam. If Adam really trusted God, he should have gone back to God to confirm whether what he had previously heard from God was what God actually told him. But Adam didn't do that. So, because of Adam's carelessness and because he failed to institute rules and standards in his home, the following calamity came upon him, his entire family and his generation yet to be born as we find in Genesis 3:8-19:

Then the man and his wife heard the sound of the LORD God as he was walking in the garden in the cool of the day, and they hid from the LORD God among the trees of the garden. But the LORD God called to the man, "Where are you?" He answered, "I heard you in the garden, and I was afraid because I was naked; so I hid." And he said, "Who told you that you were naked? Have you eaten from the tree that I commanded you not to eat from?" The man said, "The woman you put here with me—she gave me some fruit from the tree, and I ate it."

Then the LORD God said to the woman, "What is this you have done?" The woman said, "The serpent deceived me, and I ate."

So the LORD God said to the serpent, "Because you have done this, "Cursed are you above all livestock and all wild animals! You will crawl on your belly and you will eat dust all the days of your life. And I will put enmity between you and the woman, and between your offspring and hers; he will crush your head, and you will strike his heel."

To the woman he said, "I will make your pains in childbearing very severe; with painful labor you will give birth to children. Your desire will be for your husband, and he will rule over you."

To Adam he said, "Because you listened to your wife and ate fruit from the tree about which I commanded you, 'You must not eat from it,' "Cursed is the ground because of you; through painful toil you will eat food from it all the days of your life. It will produce thorns and thistles for you, and you will eat the plants of the field. By the sweat of your brow you will eat your food until you return to the ground, since from it you were taken; for dust you are and to dust you will return."

To avoid unforeseen calamities from befalling your family, you must create solid rules and standards that will keep your family members away from enemies who are on a mission to kill, steal and destroy your family. Permit me to say this: the structure you have put in place must be respected by everyone irrespective of their status. Even if the person claims to be a pastor, prophet, bishop or pope who has a word from the Lord for your child or spouse asking them to see them in their office after a Church service, protocols must be obeyed. You, as the family head, must first be told, after which the messenger must be properly vetted. If you do not find them worthy, please turn down their request without any apology. If you think they are trustworthy, please do not make the mistake of sending any member of your household without someone to accompany them. In case it concerns your spouse, you must go with her. We have seen a lot of cases where people who call themselves pastors or prophets ended up breaking lots of homes in the name of religion.

7. Create an Open Communication System

An open communication system benefits the family unit or relationship in many ways. It helps members "overcome hidden fears (Clutterbuck & Hirst, 2002:102)" such as: "Do they really accept me as a part of the union? Are they hiding any information from me? Do they perceive me in this organization as I perceive myself?" With an open communication system, members are very much open to air out issues of concerns. This, Clutterbuck & Hirst write, "reduces the build-up of hidden resistance… (Clutterbuck & Hirst, 2002:102)."

In some cultures, a wife does not have the right to bring up issues to her husband. Neither can the children do the same to their father. All this is due to the fact that the husband is regarded as the 'god' of the family unit. Since no one can address a 'god' in a direct manner, talk less of accusing the 'god' of wrongdoing, everyone chooses to shut their mouth. This attitude has split several families apart. If you are a husband that falls under this category, I encourage you to create an open atmosphere of lively discussion between you, your wife and children. Only by so doing will your family experience genuine love, trust and peace.

From the example of Adam's family we have just cited above, we can conclude that Adam did not quite have an open communication system with his wife. The reason we are saying this is because the information Eve told the serpent was not the same one God had told Adam.

Now, let us compare the original command with the one Eve told the serpent.

The original command goes (Genesis 2:16-17):

> And the LORD God commanded the man, "You are free to eat from any tree in the garden; but you must not eat from the tree of the knowledge of good and evil, for when you eat from it you will certainly die."

And here is what Eve told the serpent (Genesis 3:2):

> The woman said to the serpent, "We may eat fruit from the trees in the garden, but God did say, 'You must not eat fruit from the tree that is in the middle of the garden, and you must not touch it, or you will die.'"

Here is the problem. God never told Adam, "You must not touch it." This was an addition which could have been sorted out if there was an open communication system put in place. And this addition provided an open window for the enemy to strike. Please, ensure to always have an open communication with your spouse and children to prevent the infiltration of the enemy.

8. Manner of Approach

The approach you take will either incite or quench the fire of conflict in your family and relationships.

The right approach will always lead you to the right result. The wrong approach will invariably lead to the wrong result. No matter how good your intentions are, whenever you institute the wrong approach when dealing with a difficult issue with your spouse, be sure to get a bad result. Please, always be approach-conscious when dealing with a family crisis or when dealing with a sensitive issue that has the potential of turning into a conflict. Many conflicts, which ought not to have existed, exist today in families simply due to the fact that a wrong approach was utilized.

A 2009 study jointly conducted by Mitnick, Heyman, Malik and Smith aimed at examining the initiation of change requests and the impact pronouns made in those requests reveals the following: When husbands and wives made request for change initiated by the use of the personal pronoun, *you*, as in "You need to change …," the request was met with much resistance. However, when *you* was replaced with the third person plural, *we*, as in "We need to change …," a less resistance was met (Turner & West, 2015:100).

Why was the resistance less in the second case? It was simply because the use of "we" suggested that both partners shared the blame even if one person was to be responsible. A "we" approach will break every resistance to change in a marriage or relationship. This is one of the greatest secrets that shield conflict away from a family or relationship.

9. Be Self-controlled

When angry, count to ten before you speak.

If very angry, count to one hundred

(Thomas Jefferson, 3rd U.S. President).

By nature, humans are imperfect beings. As a result, no relationship or union formed by them is, and will ever be, perfect. Therefore, before entering into any relationship, you must be ready to bear some of the imperfections of your counterpart as they, too, bear your imperfections. And one of the ways through which this can be done is by learning how to control oneself in the face of an event that is most likely to turn into a crisis or an event that will worsen a previous crisis. One way of being self-controlled is to turn down the "mouth exit" request tendered by the words in your belly. This action alone can really save your relationship. What do you stand to gain if by spewing out those words you end up losing that relationship, which you have worked very hard to build over the years?

Do not get me wrong. I am not saying that whenever your spouse or partner or a member of your household says or does something that really annoys you, you should seal your lips and move on. I bet you, if you do practice this as a norm, it will invariably lead to a battery of petty clashes that you may probably not be able to handle anymore. On the contrary, what I am saying is that you must know when the appropriate time to speak is. Usually, we tend not to be objective in our speeches whenever we are angry. We say things only to regret a moment later. We seem to lose our mind. During the moment of anger, we are changed into a completely different person, into a person worse than our real selves.

Anger is a personality, a strange one indeed. When anger possesses the being of a man, it doesn't leave them until its purpose is achieved – the destruction of their labor. Anger is like a thief that comes upon a man *to steal* his joy, *to kill* his relationship and *to destroy* the man himself.

Come to think of it, if your action is guided by anger, you could end up losing your joy because of a broken relationship, which may ultimately result to stress and even death. That was the reason we began this section with the beautiful quote from Thomas Jefferson. Jefferson cautions us to count to ten when we are angry, and to one hundred if very angry. To some, this might seem superficial but I think it has a deep psychological significance. The only way to defeat anger is to not speak or act when anger has taken over control. This seems to be the only effective weapon against anger. Anger comes in sizes. The greater the size, the higher the count. Don't be defeated by anger; anger is too small for you. It takes only Jefferson's numerical counts of ten or one hundred to kick anger off you.

Now coming back, remember that to not speak when you are angry does not mean you will not speak at all. You should only speak when anger is gone and your sanity is restored. And it shouldn't be that moment even if you feel you have calmed down yourself. Look for another moment, preferably a day or two or even a week, depending on the situation, and talk with your spouse or whomsoever may be concerned. However, let the time for the talk not be too long as it may not have much effect in terms of producing the required results.

Note that it was anger that made God retire Moses from his life mission of delivering the people of Israel from Egypt into the Promised Land. When God told Moses to speak to the rock so that it could produce water for the thirsty people of Israel, Moses, because he was angered by the people, did strike the rock instead. As a result, Moses was barred from entering into the Promised Land, what he had labored all his entire life for (Numbers 20:2-12):

> Now there was no water for the community, and the people gathered in opposition to Moses and Aaron. They quarreled with Moses and said, "If only we had died when our brothers fell dead before the LORD! Why did you bring the LORD's community into this wilderness, that we and our livestock should die here? Why did you bring us up out of Egypt to this terrible place? It has no grain or figs, grapevines or pomegranates. And there is no water to drink!"
>
> Moses and Aaron went from the assembly to the entrance to the tent of meeting and fell facedown, and the glory of the LORD appeared to them. The LORD said to Moses, "Take the staff, and

you and your brother Aaron gather the assembly together. Speak to that rock before their eyes and it will pour out its water. You will bring water out of the rock for the community so they and their livestock can drink."

So Moses took the staff from the LORD's presence, just as he commanded him. He and Aaron gathered the assembly together in front of the rock and Moses said to them, "Listen, you rebels, must we bring you water out of this rock?" Then Moses raised his arm and struck the rock twice with his staff. Water gushed out, and the community and their livestock drank.

But the LORD said to Moses and Aaron, "Because you did not trust in me enough to honor me as holy in the sight of the Israelites, you will not bring this community into the land I give them."

Please do not let anger destroy the same thing you are building. Do not strike your children or spouse out of anger when what you are supposed to do to bring a change in them is to speak to them.

10. Let Not Outsiders Rule Your home

"If you live for the approval of others, you will die by their rejection"(Rich Warren).

One of the issues that destroy many homes is influence from outsiders. This may come from family relatives, friends or the media.

In the African context, most homes have been destroyed by the husband's mother who comes into her son's home to dictate how the home should be run. She sits at one corner of the house watching keenly as the son's wife carries out her daily matrimonial activities. When she finds that she does something or treats her son in a way that she doesn't like, she immediately rebukes her son's wife. The case is worse if the man is her only son. She is at their home not really to spend some time of fellowship with them as a mother per se but to inspect how her son is being treated. Her actions anger her son's wife, which may push the latter utter certain words that may upset her own husband. And suddenly, internal strife within the family begins, caused by the Inspector General Mother-in-law.

As an advice, as soon as you experience the drama above displayed by your mother, you should immediately talk to her letting her know she cannot intrude into your family to cause havoc. Let her know you will not tolerate such. As a husband, you owe your wife protection from whomsoever. In case you think that you love your mother so much to the extent of letting her give matrimonial orders to your wife, know that you are doing that at the detriment of your own family. Sooner or later, you will become a laughing stock to the world as your family tears apart.

As a couple, you determine the form of education of your children — public, private or home schooling. In case you have little kids, you determine whether your wife should stay at home and take care of the kids or employ the services of a baby sitter. Please avoid the 'copy and paste' syndrome. No two family structures can ever be the same. Be on your lane. As long as you stay on your family lane and drive your family carefully, you will not encounter any accidents. Safe drive!

A worthy example to mention here is the story of the Rekabite Family. This family did not allow any external influence to rule their family. They all succumbed only to the rules and regulations put in place by their forefather Jehonadab. Jehonadab ordered them never to drink wine because of the repercussions it will bring upon them.

At one time, members of the Rekabite family were asked by Jeremiah the Prophet, who, in fact, was commanded by God, to drink wine. Do you know what they did? They didn't say because Jeremiah was a trustworthy prophet they should concur to what he said. They chose to obey their forefather's instruction because it was good. They knew drinking wine would have turned them into a mess. So, they boldly turned down the prophet's request in obedience to their forefather's instruction. This story is recorded in Jeremiah 35:1-11 as shown below:

> This is the word that came to Jeremiah from the LORD during the reign of Jehoiakim son of Josiah king of Judah: "Go to the Rekabite family and invite them to come to one of the side rooms of the house of the LORD and give them wine to drink."
>
> So I went to get Jaazaniah son of Jeremiah, the son of Habazziniah, and his brothers and all his sons—the whole family of the Rekabites. I brought them into the house of the LORD, into

the room of the sons of Hanan son of Igdaliah the man of God. It was next to the room of the officials, which was over that of Maaseiah son of Shallum the doorkeeper. Then I set bowls full of wine and some cups before the Rekabites and said to them, "Drink some wine."

But they replied, "We do not drink wine, because our forefather Jehonadab son of Rekab gave us this command: 'Neither you nor your descendants must ever drink wine. Also you must never build houses, sow seed or plant vineyards; you must never have any of these things, but must always live in tents. Then you will live a long time in the land where you are nomads.' We have obeyed everything our forefather Jehonadab son of Rekab commanded us. Neither we nor our wives nor our sons and daughters have ever drunk wine or built houses to live in or had vineyards, fields or crops. We have lived in tents and have fully obeyed everything our forefather Jehonadab commanded us. But when Nebuchadnezzar king of Babylon invaded this land, we said, 'Come, we must go to Jerusalem to escape the Babylonian and Aramean armies.' So we have remained in Jerusalem."

And do you know what happened afterward? The attitude of the Rekabite family to say 'No' to things that would make them get into trouble so much pleased the Lord that the Lord had to commend their steadfastness when He said the following (Jeremiah 35:12-16):

Then the word of the LORD came to Jeremiah, saying: "This is what the LORD Almighty, the God of Israel, says: Go and tell the people of Judah and those living in Jerusalem, 'Will you not learn a lesson and obey my words?' declares the LORD. 'Jehonadab son of Rekab ordered his descendants not to drink wine and this command has been kept. To this day they do not drink wine, because they obey their forefather's command. But I have spoken to you again and again, yet you have not obeyed me. Again and again I sent all my servants the prophets to you. They said, "Each of you must turn from your wicked ways and reform your actions; do not follow other gods to serve them. Then you will live in the land I have given to you and your ancestors." But you have not paid attention or listened to me. The descendants of Jehonadab son of Rekab have carried out the command their forefather gave them, but these people have not obeyed me.'

From the above account, it clearly showed that God knew this family so well. He knew that even though He had commanded Jeremiah to tell them do what they had been forbidden from doing, they would not compromise under any circumstances. So, God used the Rekabite family as an illustration to speak to the people of Israel how obedient they should be to Him.

Your children and members of your household are what they are today because of external influences from people and particularly from the media. Like Jehonadab, you should be able to guide your children on the things they should embrace and what they are forbidden from embracing from the society. Only by so doing will your family be kept away from the intoxication of the society.

11. Let Your Spirituality Be Reflected in Your Family

The essence of belief in God or spirituality is to enable a man build his family to the standard of God. It is possible for a man to be well connected to God and yet his family is in shambles. I have worked with a few pastors whom I respected in the past only to have realized that their children were living a very wayward lifestyle. I couldn't believe my eyes. What is the essence for a man to seek God and discover God's ways and principles of living and not teach these to his own children? This is spiritual carelessness.

We all know of the man called David. David was one of the greatest men in the Bible, a man who loved God so much to the extent that he praised God seven times a day as recorded in Psalm 119:164-168:

> Seven times a day I praise you for your righteous laws. Great peace have those who love your law, and nothing can make them stumble. I wait for your salvation, LORD, and I follow your commands. I obey your statutes, for I love them greatly. I obey your precepts and your statutes, for all my ways are known to you.

David loved God to an extent that he was ready to die to protect the name of God. We all know of the famous story where David intervened at the mockery of the name of the God of Israel by Goliath the Philistine. David, a shepherd boy and an untrained soldier offered himself up to fight Goliath at a time when none of the trained soldiers of Israel was bold enough to face the giant who for forty consecutive days made mockery of the God of the Israelites.

We all know the end of the story: Goliath was defeated. David's love for God made him earn the title of "the man after God's heart" (1 Samuel 13:14).

Irrespective of whom David was, David failed to accomplish one thing: He failed to let his spirituality reflect in the lives of his children. He failed to bring up his children in the ways of the God he loved and worshipped. There are so many examples to cite. However, for reference's sake we shall cite one. This is the case of Amnon, one of David's sons, who raped his own step-sister, Tamar (2 Samuel 13:1-14):

> In the course of time, Amnon son of David fell in love with Tamar, the beautiful sister of Absalom son of David. Amnon became so obsessed with his sister Tamar that he made himself ill. She was a virgin, and it seemed impossible for him to do anything to her.
>
> Now Amnon had an adviser named Jonadab son of Shimeah, David's brother. Jonadab was a very shrewd man. He asked Amnon, "Why do you, the king's son, look so haggard morning after morning? Won't you tell me?"
>
> Amnon said to him, "I'm in love with Tamar, my brother Absalom's sister."
>
> "Go to bed and pretend to be ill," Jonadab said. "When your father comes to see you, say to him, 'I would like my sister Tamar to come and give me something to eat. Let her prepare the food in my sight so I may watch her and then eat it from her hand.'"

So Amnon lay down and pretended to be ill. When the king came to see him, Amnon said to him, "I would like my sister Tamar to come and make some special bread in my sight, so I may eat from her hand."

David sent word to Tamar at the palace: "Go to the house of your brother Amnon and prepare some food for him." So Tamar went to the house of her brother Amnon, who was lying down. She took some dough, kneaded it, made the bread in his sight and baked it. Then she took the pan and served him the bread, but he refused to eat.

"Send everyone out of here," Amnon said. So everyone left him. Then Amnon said to Tamar, "Bring the food here into my bedroom so I may eat from your hand." And Tamar took the bread she had prepared and brought it to her brother Amnon in his bedroom. But when she took it to him to eat, he grabbed her and said, "Come to bed with me, my sister."

"No, my brother!" she said to him. "Don't force me! Such a thing should not be done in Israel! Don't do this wicked thing. What about me? Where could I get rid of my disgrace? And what about you? You would be like one of the wicked fools in Israel. Please speak to the king; he will not keep me from being married to you." But he refused to listen to her, and since he was stronger than she, he raped her.

Clearly, Amnon's incest toward his step-sister, Tamar, revealed how spiritually careless David was in nurturing his children in the fear of the LORD. Please, do not separate your heart and walk with God from the education of your children. God is not simply pleased with your worship of Him. He is more pleased when you raise up a generation of worshippers like you.

12. Be Patient

For the sun to rise and the moon to fall, patience is non-negotiable.

Building a solid marital relationship and family requires a good deal of patience. You need to be much more patient with your spouse as they struggle to overcome their character challenges even as you, too, struggle to overcome yours. Remember that in the opening pages of this book we began by asserting that the family unit is not a perfect system and will never be. Being patient with one's spouse constitutes one of the greatest virtues that will save a marriage from collapse.

Most people erroneously believe that what keeps a spouse together in marriage is "love." To such people we need to ask, "What then happened to the increasing number of divorced couples today, who truly loved each other before and during the time of marriage?" You see, though love is very instrumental in marriage, love by itself does not make marriage work; work in marriage does. If you do not work your marriage while in marriage, your marriage will sooner or later crumble. Love is the engine of any relationship. However, this engine needs to be serviced for it to work properly. One way through which the love engine can be serviced is through *patience*. Patience is more feasible than love itself. When you are patient with your spouse, you send them a strong message that you love them. When you say, "I love you," your spouse does not really understand the message as they do when you are patient with them as they make mistakes. Apart from patience, the following attributes are also essential in building a solid relationship: knowledge, wisdom, kindness, gentleness and faithfulness.

BENEFITS OF QUENCHING THE CONFLICT FIRE

1. Increased Commitment

This being the case, it appears that in the management of conflict a wonderful opportunity exists to enhance effectiveness and productivity while deepening commitment to the human side of the organization (Cowan, 2003:4).

Quenching the conflict fire helps to restore the affected individual's mental soundness, which gives them the opportunity to improve their commitment within the family unit. The better the satisfaction derived from a resolved conflict, the better the quality of commitment.

2. Prevents Disruption of Interactions

Conflicts can be a great cost to a family as they are capable of slowing down or halting the family business. The conflict, for example, arising from a couple can have enormous consequences on their children, family business and extended family members. The conflict arising from a couple can affect the children's schooling dramatically. When the conflict fire is quenched, the possibility of slowing down the family business and other interactions is removed, which leads to family growth.

3. Enforcement of policies

Conflict resolution gives families the opportunity to enforce family policies, which will help to prevent further misconducts among its members. When members of the family, and outsiders, realize that the family has strengthened its policies, everyone would become more cautious of their actions.

4. Strengthens Vertical Reporting

Conflict resolution fosters or encourages vertical reporting within the family system. Investigating and resolving conflicts encourages family members to freely report any situation that distorts the system.

5. Loyalty

Conflict Resolution gives family members a good impression about their family. When family members realize that the family leadership has much interest in addressing and putting an end to matters that relate to them, they become more proud and loyal to the family.

6. Prevents Lawsuits & Divorce

Conflict resolution will save a family from divorce. Conflict resolution may also prevent the family against governmental lawsuits due to negligence in investigating and resolving conflicts (Guerin, 2007:6). The following workplace example would shed more light on this:

> Ralph was accused of sexually harassing two female coworkers. After the company carried out a thorough investigation, interviewing the two victims, Ralph, and five others whom Ralph suggested, the company found out that Ralph had sexually harassed the victims. Ralph was then fired.
>
> Ralph later sued the company under the pretext that he had a consensual affair with both victims and that they were only angry with him for two-timing them, claiming there was no sexual harassment. Ralph accused the company of unjust termination demanding damages. However, an appeals court ruled that because the company carried out a fair and thorough investigation and reached a good-faith conclusion based on the evidence

available, the company was not liable for firing Ralph (Guerin, 2007:7).

When a spouse makes an effort to reconcile their differences with their counterpart in order to resolve the family crisis at hand, such an effort is never a wasted gesture even before the court of law. Whatever be the case, the greater the efforts the better the chances of securing a positive case. Through your peaceful actions, you may restore peace into your home when reconciliation is fruitful or may be prevented from a harsh court decision.

CHAPTER 7

CONCLUSION

From our literature review, we saw a majority of the writers we contacted blacklisting conflict as the social predicament that must be dealt with if the family and relationships must function properly. To re-echo a few of these authors, Plato and Aristotle did stress that the absence of conflict is a sine qua non for the effective growth of an organization. For Elton Mayo, conflict is an evil that hampers the effectiveness of a union. Thus, conflict must be minimized or totally eliminated if the union must function properly. On the impact of conflict on one's commitment and productivity, Neuhauser writes, "Conflict is a major source of increased stress and decreased productivity for all managers and employees in any department of any organization (Rahim, 2001:2)."

We have also shown how conflict does weaken people's motivation to fully commit themselves in the family union and in other relationships. We showed how conflict injects into a union a spirit of hate, backbiting, and melancholy, all of which by transforming the union into a den similar to that of roaring lions do no good in forging the union ahead.

Can Conflict Improve One's Commitment?

All along we have been talking about quenching the conflict fire from burning within the family unit. You might be asking this question, "Is conflict not relevant for the growth of the family unit in some cases?" You are certainly right. It is. However, what kind of growth are we talking about here? A research I carried out in a Japanese manufacturing company reveals this type of growth to be *cosmetic* in nature. I hereby present some of the findings of that research here-below:

The research findings revealed that workplace conflicts do hinder workers' performances. Sixty percent (60%) of the Case Study Participants (CSPs) did acknowledge that there was little or no improvement in their performance during the conflict interval. The other forty percent (40%) could not really tell.

During the interview phase, one of the CSPs indicated that the conflict he had with their supervisor during work operations had actually challenged him to improve his performance. When I asked to know why, he said that he did that for the mere purpose of saving his job. Here is the twist: the CSP in question actually confided in this researcher that the conflict had actually pushed him to go look for a job elsewhere, and that when he must have secured one, he would retaliate to the maltreatment imposed on him by their supervisor by assaulting the said supervisor in the presence of other co-workers. Therefore, the improved performance that might have been witnessed with the naked eyes was a cosmetic one, it was a camouflage.

The same is true for conflicts within the family unit. When someone's commitment tends to increase even though they are being consumed inside by the conflict fire, it is a gross error to take this scenario as a sign of growth, order and stability. No sane person can actually make any production from a pit of fire unless the production is meant to enable them come out of the fire.

It is not uncommon to find the above scenario today in many marriages and relationships. Many women undergo all manner of abuses and maltreatments, yet instead of looking for a way to solve the problem, they choose to go extra miles to please their husband so as to attract their husband's attention. Does attracting one's attention take out the prevailing conflict? No. This is nothing but a cosmetic surgery, which will sooner or later be peeled off. And when this peeling-off happens, the woman would have no way to hide.

We also saw all the sacrifices that David made in trying to please King Saul to have the king change his mind and not pursue David. Saul pretended to have changed his mind and David thought his relationship with the king had been restored only for King Saul to recommence his project for the assassination of David a while later. Why? Because no healthy relationship can ever be formed while the fire of conflict burns.

In a marriage relationship, as long as the bitterness abides, the conflict afflicts. As long as the conflict afflicts and the affliction becomes unbearable the wife becomes overly fed up to the point where she suddenly quits the relationship. This is the worst scenario of any conflict. Conflict must not, for any reasons, be left to graduate to this level. At this level, it is almost impracticable to quench the conflict fire as the victim of the conflict has woefully made up their mind and turned their back against the offender and the union. To them, going back to the union is similar to a journey into the lake of fire. Therefore, at this stage, anyone who tries to persuade them into going back into that union is perceived as an enemy who must be fought at all cost.

Thomas Edison once said that "Our greatest weakness lies in giving up." You may be at the point of almost giving up on your spouse, children, family and relationships. Please, don't. All the troubles and failures you have had in those relationships are meant to make you, not to mock you. Perhaps, they are meant to make you meek, which was what was lacking in you. There is still hope for you. I am happy to let you know that you are not alone. Many others are going through similar and even worse situations. Do not worry for "worry is a misuse of the imagination" as Dan Zadra tells us. I encourage you not to give up.

Let me briefly share with you the experience of Thomas Edison during his experiments. In trying to come up with the first efficient filament-based light bulb, we are told Edison did fail 10,000 times. This is where the story gets interesting. When asked about his failures, Edison is quoted to have responded by saying that he didn't fail, but that he only learned 10,000 ways of what not to do to invent a filament-based light bulb. Like Edison, for all these years you have learned what you shouldn't do to have a joyful and fulfilled family life and relationships. So, with the knowledge you now have, I encourage you to rise up now to restore peace, joy, love, unity, order and stability into your family and relationships by quenching the conflict fire. Restore your family and relationships now to prevent heavy, painful and unbearable losses in the future. Good luck.

REFERENCES

Anolli, L., Duncan Jr., S., Magnusson, M.S., and Riva, G. (Eds.). (2005). *The Hidden Structure of Interaction: From Neurons to Culture Patterns*. Amsterdam: IOS Press.

Avruch, K. (1998). *Culture and Conflict Resolution*. Washington: United States Institute of Peace Press.

Bacon, F. (2000). *The New Organon*. Lisa Jardine and Michael Silverthorne. (Eds.). UK: Cambridge University Press.

Bacon, Francis. *The New Organon: The True Directions Concerning the Interpretations of Nature, LII. Retrieved from* http://books.google.co.jp/books?id=hTbE_UHvWg8C&printsec=frontc over#v=onepage&q&f=false

Bryman, A., Collinson, D., Grint, K., Jackson, B., and Uhl-Bien, M. (Eds.). (2011). *The SAGE Handbook of Leadership*. London: SAGE Publications.

Buckley, W.R. and Okrent, C.J. (2004). *Torts & Personal Injury Law*. (3rd Ed.). Canada: Thomson Delmar Learning.

Clutterbuck, D., and Hirst, S. (2002). *Talking Business: Making Communication Work*. UK: The Item Group Ltd.

Colbert, D. (2003). *Deadly Emotions: Understand the Mind-Body-Spirit Connection that can Heal or Destroy You*. Nashville: Thomas Nelson, Inc.

Coombs, C.H., and Avrunin, G.S. (1988). *The Structure of Conflict*. New Jersey: Lawrence Erlbaum Associates, Inc.

Cooper, T.D. (2003). *Sin, Pride & Self-Acceptance: The Problem of Identity in Theology & Psychology*. USA: Inter Varsity Press.

Cowan, D. (2003). *Taking Charge of Organizational Conflict: A Guide to Managing Anger and Confrontation*. USA: Personhood Press.

Darwin, C. (2007). *The Expression of the Emotions in Man and Animals*. Teddington: The Echo Library.

Darwin, C. (2007). *The Expression of the Emotions in Man and Animals*. Teddington: The Echo Library.

De Dreu, C.K.W., and Beersma, B. (Eds.). (2005). *Conflict in Organizations: Beyond Effectiveness and Performance.* UK: Psychology Press Ltd.

Gerzon, M. (2006). *Leading through Conflict: How Successful Leaders Transform Differences into Opportunities.* USA: Harvard Business School Press.

Guerin, L. (2007). *The Essential Guide to Workplace Investigations.* USA: Nolo.

Hines, D.L. (2002). *Resolving conflict in Marriage.* USA: Whitaker House.

Hodgkinson, C. (1991). *Educational Leadership: The Moral Art.* USA: State University of New York Press.

Knapp, M.L., and Daly, J.A. (Eds.). (2002). *Handbook of Interpersonal Communication.* (3rd Ed.). USA: Sage Publications, Inc.

Lehman, C.M., and Dufrene, D.D. (2010). *Business Communication.* (16th Ed.). USA: Cengage Learning.

Nicotera, A.M. (Ed.). (1995). *Conflict and Organizations: Communicative Processes.* Albany: State University of New York Press.

Oade, A. (2009). *Managing Workplace Bullying: How to Identify, Respond to and Manage Bullying Behaviour in the Workplace.* UK: Palgrave Macmillan.

Rahim, M.A. (Ed.). (2001). *Managing Conflict in Organizations*. USA:

Greenwood Publishing Group.

Richardson, R.W. (2010). *Couples in Conflict: A Family Systems Approach

to Marriage Counseling*. USA: Fortress Press.

Samovar, L.A., Porter, R.E., McDaniel, E.R., and Roy, C.S. (2010).

Communication between Cultures. (7th Ed.). Canada: Cengage

Learning.

Sashkin, M., and Sashkin, M.G. (2003). *Leadership that Matters: The

Critical Factors for Making a Difference in People's Lives and

Organizations' Success*. USA: Berrett- Koehler Publishers, Inc.

Turner, L. H., and West, R. (Eds.). (2015). The SAGE Handbook of

Family Communication. USA: SAGE.

ABOUT THE AUTHOR

Njikang Clovis Mebinaji is a charismatic and passionate solution-oriented thinker whose life ambition is to assist men and women of all calibers come out of the challenges that plague humanity. He hails from Cameroon and is the 13th child in a polygamous family of 17. He holds a doctor's degree in Religious Education, an International Master in Business Administration (IMBA), a BA in Liberal Arts and a B.Sc. in Accountancy. He has previously served as an accountant and spiritual guardian. Presently, he teaches in two Japanese public schools. Mebinaji is happily married to Catherine.